The Healing Woman

A Beginner's Guide to Healing the Feminine Mind, Body, and Soul

Introduction

We are all on a path of healing. We are all at some point on the continuum between sick and well. To be engaged in healing is to be in our natural condition. As human animals, we are built to continually maintain, repair, and improve all aspects of our being.

The roots of the word 'heal' relate to the idea of wholeness or making whole. Every aspect of our daily existence, the aches and twinges in our physical body, that persistent niggling worry that comes to mind, the occasional inspiration or strange dream we have, and the surging tides of emotion that flow through us: these are all healing in action. They are the signs from our inner being saying, "Hey you, look at this!" Sometimes they are pointing out things we need to fix. Sometimes they are just things we need to know.

In the great mystery of life, by some sort of unfathomable mechanism of the universe, what happens around us is part of the healing. This might be our family, our relationships, our work, our neighborhood, or the state of the nation mirroring to us the problems and solutions to the issues we are working through. Yup, I mean even that weird knocking in your car engine, the nasty remark the cashier made at the grocery store, and the pair of swans gliding on the lake in the park yesterday. Every aspect of your being and life itself is conspiring to nudge you towards wholeness and health. Ideally, you are in on this too.

If you are reading this, at some level you are saying, "Something has to change." This book is a compendium of catalysts for change. These are things you can try to move things along in your healing journey.

Think of it like a big virtual bran tub. Do they still have those? They are the big barrels of, well, bran, that they have at fetes and fairs where you plunge in your hand and pull out a gift. It might be a toy or a bag of sweets or a sachet of pot-pourri. Where do you even get bran?

We have arranged the gifts in this book after a fashion, but it is not necessary to work through the book from beginning to end, although I suppose you could. Perhaps there are some things you already know. Some will make you roll your eyes, and some will delight you so much, they will change your life. By the way, do try a couple of the things you roll your eyes at. They might surprise you. They are small side steps out of your comfort zone.

I am writing this at a time of a global pandemic. We are all adjusting to an unappealing new world of face masks, hand sanitizer and the so-called "social distancing," which is not very social at all. It has given many of us the opportunity to pause and reflect on our lives, to realize what is working for us and what is not, and to ponder "what it all means." We are experiencing the effects of the famous Chinese curse: "May you live in interesting times." But the Chinese character for 'crisis' also contains the form of the character for "opportunity." COVID-19 is our opportunity for changing things. Take your opportunity to consciously participate in your own healing process.

It is not just about healing your body, although that is *always* part of the story. It is about working with your mind and thoughts too, in fact getting them to work for you. It is about riding our emotional waves and seeing those unruly disturbances for the precious gifts they are. It is about inviting and encouraging those sparks of inspiration that illuminate our lives and creating a situation where more and more of them are attracted: whole firework parties of 'em.

The Healing Woman is about changing your world by changing yourself and persuading yourself to make better choices. A friend of mine, bemoaning the trials of 2020, sent me a cartoon with a character hanging from a cliff top by a thin branch. The comment was, "Always remember, no matter how bad things seem, they can always get worse!" Maybe this is a bit too true for you right now to enjoy the dark humor. But of course, things can always get better too. A Buddhist monk once told me when I was feeling incredibly sad, that as sad as I felt then, I was assuredly capable of experiencing an equal and opposite height of joy. It is true.

I am personally rather dubious about the slippery concept of "happiness." It conjures the picture of the women in 1950s and 1960s advertising images radiantly grinning as they scrubbed floors. Not that one cannot enjoy washing a floor, but those images had an unreal, manic quality, a "Stepford Wives" vibe. If someone is feeling this way all the time, they are either a spiritual master, probably reading an ancient sutra rather than this, or else, something is wrong.

When I was in college, there was a fashion for posters with beautiful images of nature with inspiring words of wisdom. Think of blue distant hills at twilight and the legend: "Tomorrow is Another Day." One that has really stuck with me was a picture of a cute duckling standing and staring square on, on his huge and silly orange feet. Round brown eyes looked over the beak, knowing and penetrating and redolent of more "old soul" wisdom that I expected in a duckling. The legend was, "Happiness is an inside job." It might have been my first inkling that life did not just happen to me, that my actions and, especially, my attitudes could change everything. Be a wise duckling, jump in and try to change things!

Chapter 1: Elementary

Once, things in the world were classified as pertaining to either Fire, Water, Air, or Earth. It was wildly popular in medieval times and up to the 17th century. At that time, doctors used these distinctions, seeing their patients' constitutions and the remedies they used in these terms.

A person's 'humors' (body fluids/essences) and their characteristic balance of these qualities governed their 'temperament.' People were more or less fiery (choleric), watery (phlegmatic), earthy (melancholic), or airy (sanguine). This described their physiology and indicated the medicines appropriate for them and for addressing the particular malady that ailed them. It also determined the qualities of their personality and even appearance. You will notice that the temperaments persist in our language describing characteristic ways of being.

All the physicians of those olden days had to be astrologers. An astrological birth chart clearly shows a person's elemental or temperamental make-up. Although few physicians today use these distinctions, elemental bias is still a brilliant shorthand for discussing the subtle differences of energies and the nature of phenomena.

Fiery things are fast and furious, instinctive, and assertive, if not aggressive. Fiery energy also relates to inspiration. Fiery people are action men and women. They want to get up and be at it, whatever it is. Flames are hot: they can burn and destroy, but they also have the power to transform materials and forge new substances. Fiery energy is a key aspect of creativity. It arises spontaneously within us and demands to be expressed. Fiery energy is focused. It is instinctive.

The watery quality has to do with feeling and emotion. It is the watery quality that connects us to inspiration, to our unconscious, and to the collective unconscious. Water energy is reflective and flowing and resists containment. Although it feels gentle, watery energy is powerful. Think of the ability of a mountain to carve a deep, plunging valley through the rock and earth of a mountain.

Earth is a slower, steadier energy that relates to what is real. Earth energy deals with tangible things, the things we can smell, touch, taste, feel, and hear. Earth energy, in tandem with our senses, connects us to our beautiful world and the realms of nature. It is where we get 'grounded.' Earth energy is determined and a tad stubborn. Think of the famous tortoise who won the race against the over-confident hare.

Air energy is how we connect. It relates to the world of thoughts and ideas. Airy energy is how we connect to others by talking and writing and the new medium of the internet. Air is energy is another fast-moving energy. It is idealistic and builds bridges between people, and bridges between people and ideas.

In this book, we have gathered healing suggestions into those that speak to the Fire, Water, Earth, or Air energies. Almost certainly, you will find one or two of these elements more appealing than others. This is an expression of your natural, inborn elemental bias. You would see this made explicit in an astrological reading from a competent professional astrologer, if such a thing appealed to you.

If two elemental energies are interacting, think in a very literal way how they might work together. I am a water and air type person: water and air in combination suggests 'bubbles,' giving qualities of enthusiasm and the capacity to be frivolous or humorous alternatively 'fog,' which can be confusing and unclear and mysterious. Air and fire give the idea of "fanning the flames" or 'wildfire,' both very dynamic and out-of-control energies with the capacity for destruction or burn-out, but certainly not boring. Earth and water give us mud, at first sight a little prosaic and unappealing, but consider that mud is where life comes from, from the plants we eat to the primordial ooze from which we all emerged. Also, "where there's muck, there's brass," as the English saying has it: it is an energy with the potential to inspire financial gain. Fire and water are not comfortable together. We see fire put out and water boiled away; but with some impressive whistling, hissing, and spitting in the process. Get the idea? The thing is that, while respecting your energetic temperament, it is good to try some healing modalities from all the sections. Although one elemental energy predominates, we are all, or we all should be, a mixture of all these energies.

Those physicians of yesteryear ascribed all disease to an imbalance of the 'humors." The humors were the bodily fluids associated with the various temperaments. Fiery, 'choleric' individuals have a predominance of "yellow bile;" watery, 'phlegmatic' people of phlegm; earthy 'melancholics' of "black bile;" and airy 'sanguine' folk of blood. Their healing practice sought to bring these humors into balance.

A holistic healing approach today seeks to bring energies into balance. It wants to help individuals to give expression to all life areas. Fire is our active, creative, instinctual self. Earth is our practical, responsible, grounded, and realistic self. Water is our contemplative, reflective, emotional, 'inner' self. Air is our communicative, expansive, relational self. In healing, we are trying to make sure we are firing smoothly on all these cylinders.

Chapter 2: Female, Feminine, and The Feminine

P eople go to college for four years to unravel these terms. Here, we will see what we can do to differentiate these ideas in four pages.

Female and Feminine

THE PHILOSOPHER SIMONE de Beauvoir explained that no one was born a woman, but instead became one (de Beauvoir, 1949). She meant that what we understand by woman or girl was largely socially and culturally determined. We are raised to behave like women and girls. Certainly, we all know what we mean by female and recognize new babies as either girls or boys. There is of course more understanding these days of the relatively few individuals who are born "in between" with characteristics of both sexes, now termed 'intersex.' Previously, intersex people might have been called hermaphrodites, but that is now considered a negative and stigmatizing nomenclature. They suffered appalling discrimination and ill treatment. Similarly, there is more assistance today for people born one sex but feeling that they want to be different, and they are sometimes supported to change sex if they wish. Certainly, transsexual people have many challenges, even in more open and tolerant societies, but things are changing in the right direction.

Femininity is a concept that encompasses all the various characteristics and attributes that are typically associated with women and girls. It is a social construct influenced by biology. Feminine traits include gentleness and agreeableness, sensitivity and empathy, kindness and docility and warmth. Critics of the 'patriarchal' cultures of the past 2000 years considered that society drove an association of femininity with less positive characteristics like frailty, fearfulness, shyness, and incompetence, and cast women as ornamental and precious creatures who were not effective or capable of valuable work or contributions, leadership, or decision-making. Gender identity develops early in life, and it is a "cultural dimension."

Of course, particular cultures and social classes modify these images. I had two grandmothers who lived through two world wars that were probably instrumental in them stepping out of the generally prescribed woman's role. Both worked throughout their lives, despite bearing and raising large families, one a businesswoman running a small hotel, the other a teacher. They were enabled by being surrounded by large, close-knit families who shared childcare and domestic duties. Poor women and rural women frequently took on extremely hard work, until recently with little recompense and certainly little control over their own lives.

In over a century of rapid and accelerating social change, we have seen women's lives change dramatically. Women today have agency and opportunity way beyond the imaginings of their grandmothers. These have benefits and challenges. While it is generally believed that women have greater freedom and power now, they are still subject to social pressures and internalized imperatives to do certain things and behave in particular ways.

Young women are encouraged to embrace their educational and career opportunities and prove themselves the equal of men in all ways. This goes very well until the biology of reproduction intervenes. Following the natural instinct to become mothers and create families creates a hiatus in women's lives. Interruptions to career progress are often never "made up," and the dual demands of parenting and work life are onerous and leave many feeling overwhelmed and that they are failing both spheres. Our enlightened times are supposed to mean that childcare is shared by parents (as are domestic tasks), but in reality women often still take on most of this work. The freedom and ability to control their destiny given by effective birth control, especially since the advent of "the pill" in the 1960s actually leaves women with acute dilemmas. To be a mother at all? To delay childbearing until it is "almost too late," which has its own dangers and difficulties? To forgo the joys of "being there," for their growing offspring as they work long hours to provide materially for them is to the detriment of both parties in many cases. When families break up, it is nearly always the mother who is left the "lone parent," with all the stress, privations, and social stigma that carries.

Caitlin Moran, an Irish writer, comedian, and columnist, wrote a memoir called *How to Be a Woman* which has sold millions of copies. It uses humor to elucidate the absurdities and contradictions of contemporary women's lives. It also doesn't shy away from the poignant tragedies that occur: "You can tell whether some misogynistic societal pressure is being exerted on women by calmly enquiring: 'Are men doing this as well?' If they are not, chances are you are dealing with what we strident feminists refer to as 'some total f***ing bullshit" (Moran, 2011).

This book was criticized by some feminist intellectuals on various points, but it resonated with millions of people and it made them laugh uproariously. Humor is a potent weapon for change. The book is a bit swear-y, but 'bad' language has a powerful impact too, used in the right way.

The Feminine

WITH THE ADDITION OF the definite article, here we are in another dimension altogether. The feminine is related to and associated with women and girls, but not essentially about them.

The feminine is a more abstract archetypal energy. There are general universal energies of which we are more or less aware, depending on how tuned in we are to the "collective unconscious," as Jung named his the great repository of shared deep beliefs and instinctive understandings common to all mankind. In the collective unconscious we encounter the ideas or 'archetypes' of primal things like The Mother or The Shadow or The Trickster, or even Fire, Water, Earth, and Air discussed earlier.

There is The Feminine and The Masculine. These get translated into the idea of gender, but they have their own wider and more universal meanings. Concepts of the feminine and the masculine are important in the teaching of major religions and esoteric belief systems. Different beliefs personify and explore the divine feminine and the divine masculine and imbue them with characteristics.

Masculine and feminine are a pair of polar opposites, and two opposite archetypes are vibrationally linked. In a way, the existence of The Masculine depends on the existence of The Feminine and vice versa. Each contains the "potentiality of the other." Eastern philosophy gave us Yin and Yang as expressions of The Feminine and The Masculine. They also gave the eloquent symbol of the 'Taijitu.' This Yin-Yang symbol shows how the dark contains the seed of the light and they are in a fluid balance. The two polarities are interdependent and interpenetrating.

Concepts of the feminine and the masculine are important in the teaching of major religions and esoteric belief systems. Different beliefs personify and explore the divine feminine and the divine masculine and imbue them with characteristics.

The Masculine is Yang, light, logic, and action. The Feminine is Yin, darkness, intuition, receptivity, and creativity.

Jung introduced the idea of the Anima and the Animus. The Anima is the feminine personality within men, and the Animus is the masculine personality within women. We all contain both polarities, and unless we develop and express these energies, we are out of balance.

None of us, of course, are in perfect balance with respect to any of our inner polar energies. Life is about responding and adjusting to a fluid and shifting balance of the energies, in response to people and experiences in the outer world or the prompting of our inner being, seeking to restore balance. Health is about keeping the inner energies balanced.

The spiritual writer Deganit Nuur writes online about restoring the balance in our inner masculine and feminine energies, recognizing first our constitutional predisposition to a particular imbalance (Nuur, n.d.). She explains how to identify if your nature is predisposed to being a little bit or a lot more Yin or Yang, how that imbalance can destabilize your spirit, and actions to take to redress the balance.

As women we would seek to honor and celebrate the feminine in a way contemporary culture has failed to do, but to achieve health and wholeness and a strong feminine energy, we must address, honor, and celebrate the masculine within too. Incidentally, the Fire and Air elements discussed are archetypally masculine energies. Earth and Water are archetypally feminine.

That is enough theory. Let us jump in now and start exploring and doing.

Chapter 3: Fire: Keep 'Er Lit

In the North of Ireland, there is a colloquial phrase: "Keep 'er lit." It would be addressed to a friend or colleague perhaps and carry the meaning "keep on" (with whatever you might be doing) or "keep going!" and imply encouragement and approval. I think it also has a deeper level of unspoken encouragement: Keep the spark alive, keep the passion and the meaning alive. Less explicit but more fervent and, well, loving. How interesting that the flame, the spark, the fire they refer to is designated 'her' ('er).

The Fire section will include things that pertain to the ideas of action, strength, challenge, intuition, drive, and enthusiasm. For instance, Kinesiology is here because it works with the *power* of *muscles*.

You can drag and drop here in the Fire section anything that you absolutely love to do, anything that inspires passion, because that feeds your fire and is definitely healing. Have you abandoned or strayed from these things? Has life got in the way of your skateboarding, acting, embroidery, writing or something else that you always loved to do? Find practices here to bring you back to those joyous activities.

I hope the suggestions here feed your fire, spark enthusiasm and encourage you to connect with the passion and generally "keep 'er lit."

Mind

Competition

ARE YOU A COMPETITIVE person? Fiery individuals typically are. Perhaps the idea of competition fills you with dread but stay with me here. A little competition can be good for everyone.

Whatever activity you are engaging in—sports, work, writing poetry—adding the spice of competition can help you develop skills more quickly. It is motivating and forces you to evaluate your strengths and weaknesses and make a plan to succeed.

Workplace managers know that introducing competition adds to productivity, and people are encouraged to stretch to their full potential. In doing so, they learn things about themselves, others, and their relationships.

Of course, it does not work very well if people are unhealthily competitive, focused on winning at all costs, and worst of all, taking delight in putting others down or even cheating. Poor players cannot handle the disappointment of not winning and pout like frustrated toddlers.

Well handled, competition is a positive motivation, helps us develop skills, and teaches us about how we personally handle stress. We learn to "meet with triumph and disaster and treat those two imposters just the same," as it says in Kipling's poem 'If' (Kipling, 1910).

Suppose you enjoy writing poems. The idea of entering a competition motivates you to complete and perfect a piece of work. It might stretch you by suggesting a topic or form unfamiliar to you. Having to have your work ready by a certain date is an automatic goal. If you win, great, and if you do not win, you can analyze your work and that of the winners and see where you might improve. Or you might realize that your poem was perfect and should have won, the judges got it wrong. In any case, the competition was useful and productive.

What if you are starting to run daily? It might be fun to join a park run or local running group. The competition is low key, and you will meet other people enjoying doing the same thing. It might just motivate you to get out there on a gray, miserable day when you do not really feel like it. If you really love competition, then maybe you will train for a marathon. Competition can foster goal setting and planning, encourage people to take positive risks and imbue one with *persistence*. These are all the ingredients for success in any field, and perhaps the goals are transferable. You can learn them in a non-threatening way at your local swimming club and apply them in your career.

There is a wider benefit too. If you engage in competition, you up the performance across the whole field of endeavor, whether it is sales targets at work, raising money for a charity at a bake sale, or bringing back a medal for your judo club as well as yourself. The best healthy competitors encourage others. They want to bring on and develop the competition they love to have around them.

So, whatever you are trying to do, consider if a little competition could give you an edge.

Creativity

DID YOU SEE THIS AND assume I am about to advocate watercolor painting or crocheting covers for toilet paper rolls? Well, those things could be fabulous, but I am thinking more in general here. Not about creativity applied and expressed in one skill, but about the general attitude and capacity of creativity that we can bring to bear in any aspect of life.

Creativity is applied imagination. It is where we come up with new ideas and solutions to problems. It is where we bring ideas together and solve problems with a unique combination. It is creativity that helps us find a new way to communicate to others, how we are feeling or what we know about something. Creativity famously is at the root of entertainment. If we live a creative life, we entertain ourselves with interesting ideas.

Creativity is a capacity we all have. Some people believe our innate creativity is dampened by aspects of our education and socialization. Creativity needs us to be (allowed to be) curious and willing to experiment and to try to see things in new ways.

There was a popular book called *Drawing with the Right Side of the Brain* which was written by an art teacher with an interest in neuroscience and creativity (Edwards, 1979). It relates to the fact that the two hemispheres of our brain process information differently. The left side of the brain relates to logic, verbalization, and analytic thought. The right side of the brain processes visual, spatial, and perceptual information. The right side of the brain was characterized as "creative." Most people are right-handed, and this reflects a dominance of the left brain. This book showed some methods using drawing to stimulate the development of the left brain and thus enhance creativity.

Another highly influential creative method was described in Julia Cameron's book *The Artist's Way* (Cameron, 1992). It gives a 12-week program of activity designed to liberate creative potentials. It is beloved of 'blocked' writers and painters. I found it difficult to read, resenting that less than optimal creativity was being deemed pathological and that I needed 'curing.' However, I persisted and for me, as for others, her prescribed method worked. It includes "morning pages", three pages of unedited longhand written on waking every day, and a weekly "artist's date", at least two hours alone being somewhere or doing something inspiring, be it visiting the Uffizi, coloring with dollar store crayons, or wandering in the Botanic Gardens. Despite my misgivings, *The Artist's Way* worked for me, more than once. Six weeks of religiously observed morning pages will infallibly unearth some surprising new idea or burst of creativity. So now morning pages are part of my life. Even if I bridled at the preachy "12-step" tone, I agreed how perfectionism and the dreaded "inner critic" kills your creativity. It's for all sorts of creatives, not just writers.

Goal Setting

GOAL SETTING IS HOW successful and effective people get stuff done. They have a clear vision of what they want to do and a clear plan of how they are getting there. Thinking vaguely that "one day I will grow vegetables" is not the way to get succulent tomatoes and ultra-fresh spinach in your sandwich.

The obvious first step is thinking, "What do I really want?" Do you have an idea where you want to be in five years (as they used to ask people at job interviews)? If something is not right, what do you want to change? If something is missing, what is it and how do you get it?

If you want to get more fit, you need an action plan. Just thinking about it obviously won't work, but neither will dashing out impetuously and buying lycra, then trying to achieve something unrealistic and getting dejected. I purchased some yoga DVDs, but sitting on my bedroom windowsill for a month, they were quite useless. What do you want to achieve? Do you want to fit into a certain outfit for a special occasion or get "swimsuit fit"? Do you want to lose a certain amount of weight? Do you want to establish a sustainable, ongoing fitness regimen, or do you want to achieve a sports goal or be "match fit" for some competition?

Once you have your goal in mind, then you come up with a plan. You break the big goal into small and manageable goals.

You will have heard of 'SMART' objectives. These are the criteria for goals that have the best chance of being met. SMART usually stands for specific, measurable, attainable, relevant, and time bound. Some people substitute significant, meaningful, actionable, rewarding, and trackable, which are a bit different but also useful.

So, specifically, your 'fit' might include losing weight and increasing cardiovascular health. You might set a goal of losing 30 pounds, being able to run up the stairs in your apartment building or being able to jog for an hour if that is realistic for you. You put a timeframe on the plan, say six months. It is important that you can measure your progress, so what do you weigh now and how far can you run now? Your objectives must be measurable, and those objectives have to be relevant to your overall goal of fitness.

It is generally a good idea to write down goals and their SMART objectives. Better still, communicate to a friend. This cements your commitment, because now someone will know if you do not carry through.

Perhaps your vision is to achieve a higher and better paid role in your organization. Perhaps you see yourself in your line manager's role, in two to three years. How can you make progress towards this? Thinking this through will generate your goals. Are there skills you need to develop or courses you can take to enhance your chances? Are there responsibilities you can take on to demonstrate your leadership and management ability? Can you enhance relationships in the workplace and find a mentor? Working through your action plan of SMART objectives puts you in a brilliant position to point out your particular achievements, contributions and professional development efforts at the next employment review. You can then ask for more opportunity and responsibility.

Perhaps you want to leave your job and become self-employed, start a business, or make money from your creativity. Once again, think of the first steps you can take: Further learning that can improve your skills, learning about the practicalities of tax reporting and budgeting for your own company, developing a website, finding helpful organizations you can join, seeking a mentor or planning a period of transitional 'moonlighting' to test your readiness to switch. Then set the time scales and work out how you will measure your achievement.

Ticking off your action plan goals gives a sense of progress, achievement, and pride, and builds your self-confidence. Expect to trip up at some point. Is it taking too long? Perhaps you need to further break down that goal into something more attainable. Have you realized there is a skill gap? One by one, you kick aside the obstacles. Remind yourself from time to time of your big vision and celebrate the progress you are making.

Goals can be big things or small things, but setting goals can keep you focused and on track and in the way of turning dreams into reality.

Body

Keep Moving

WE ALL KNOW WE ARE supposed to be doing daily exercise. There are various guidelines for the amount of times or how often you should be raising your heart rate. It's not just extending your life but enhancing your quality of life. I am not one of life's natural gym bunnies. The gym is fabulous, of course, if you like that sort of thing, especially if weight training and sculpting your body in that way appeals. The camaraderie and motivation and fun of fitness classes is brilliant, but it is not for everyone. Horses for courses, as they say. However, there is definitely a kind of exercise out there to suit you.

Exercise keeps our heart and circulation system healthy, strengthens our muscles, keeps our joints flexible and makes sure our breath delivers oxygen effectively to our organs and muscles. It also helps our bodies release endorphins, the feel-good endocrine secretions, so our mental and emotional health as well as physical health is supported. It is often hard to begin. As children, we naturally want to move and delight in being very active and stretching and challenging our bodies. Life tethers us to chairs in schools, offices, and commuter trains. Unless we make a conscious choice, exercise can easily disappear from life. Once you do bring it back, it becomes a source of pleasure and an indispensable aid to wellbeing, not a chore anymore.

I would always rather be outside, even if it is raining, which is frequently the case where I live. An ill-managed schedule with long office hours and a car commute left me very unfit and shaped rather like a seal. A new job offered me the opportunity to control my schedule, and I was astounded by what just an hour of daily walking could achieve. Aches and pains that were annoying, although not serious enough to send me to a doctor, magically disappeared. I was more flexible, slim, and energetic than I had been in years in a matter of weeks. I soon added in an evening bicycle ride, and frequently I could not resist another little stroll before bedtime. I had all the joy of time to appreciate my surroundings, the change of seasons, and the chance to chat and wave to my neighbors; it was ticking a lot of boxes. I changed my route to include a particularly steep hill, which feels like a mini achievement every day. It is my personal daily Everest.

Perhaps your taste will be for something more energetic and ambitious. Are you a runner? Worldwide "Couch to 5K" programs have worked for people who thought they weren't. "Park Run" participation adds companionship and a bit of friendly competition while tracking your performance and progress. You can walk a Park Run, push a stroller, or try to keep up with your dog.

Want to fuse your daily movement with art and self-expression? If you have access to a dance studio, a few dance lessons a week are a brilliant workout. I once experimented with dance lessons. I loved ballet, living out little girl fantasies of grace and femininity, although I was probably more fairy elephant than prima ballerina. Perhaps your personality lends itself more to jazz or modern dance. Try a taster class and see. Then you can dance with others, of course. Are you "strictly ballroom," or are you seduced by the Latin rhythms of salsa, flamenco, or tango? African dance or street and hip-hop is exuberantly energetic. Capoeira from Brazil exotically combines the fluidity and elegant expression of dance with martial arts moves and music.

Yoga is a holistic movement practice that unites mind, body and spirit. It is discussed below in the soul section but belongs here too.

Do you enjoy sports? Taking part, I mean. This is the place for those individuals who thrive on competition, and sports have a brilliant socially interactive side. I never fared well with team sports. I fear perhaps I am not really a "team player" by nature and always suspected my distaste of the team games at school reflected a character flaw. I did love those individual practice sports like swimming and archery. Are you a rugged individualist or a pillar of the squad?

Swimming is the sport that uses your whole body. For people with injuries, the water helps support your weight as you exercise, so it is easy on your hips and knees. Archery is fun, mostly of course an upper body practice, and you can connect with your inner Lord Of the Rings "elf-self."

With a tight schedule or wanting to begin in the privacy of your own home, you can follow exercise and yoga videos or DVDS. I enjoyed a short DVD which taught an 18-minute sequence of qigong and tai chi movements. It was very invigorating and freeing. When I lost the disc, I was bereft, but found I was able to carry out the practice by myself. My body had learned the sequence in that mysterious 'body-memory' way, and it was now part of me. The DVD was *The Barefoot Doctor's Tai Chi Workout* by the late Stephen Russell (Russell, 2007). I loved that it ascribed emotional and psychological healing effects to the movements that I could tailor to my own concerns. That simple short exercise sequence was something I could squeeze into any short break. It inspired me to join Tai Chi classes eventually, which I also enjoyed.

Horse riding of course includes the blessing of interacting with another species and is very good exercise too. Staying in calm and gentle control of the horse by the assertive expression of your will is a life skill, probably why learning to ride early in life is said to be "character-building." I love horses, but I am a hopeless rider. Deep down, I don't see why any creature should do what I say (and I don't like to take orders myself much either); perhaps horses sense this, or perhaps I lack the requisite "character." I believe anything that gets you out in the fresh air, especially in natural surroundings, is such a blessing, availing of the natural healing of clean fresh air and light.

In the right climate, you can try downhill or cross-country skiing or the increasingly popular walking with "Nordic poles." If you are lucky enough to live by a body of water, there are all sorts of aquatic sports: Sailing and surfing and paddle boarding and windsurfing, rowing, and messing about on the river in kayaks and canoes. Divers can also pierce the surface and explore beneath, with scuba or deep diving equipment and more bravery that I possess!

Access to the right facilities or the expense of the equipment may prohibit your participation in some kinds of exercise or limit it to holiday-time activity. But walking is available to everyone. Walking is very special, something humans have evolved to do. It moves your muscles and stimulates and caresses internal organs aiding digestion and elimination, and it also does something strange in your brain. Writers and painters and other creatives frequently cite the importance of a daily walk for processing information and allowing solutions to naturally appear. If you cannot think of how to do something, a walk can be as effective as "sleeping on it."

If you have a dog, you have a wonderful companion who will be your excuse to go for a walk a few times a day, as well as an unconditionally loving best friend. They also introduce you to other dog walkers and widen your social circle.

Whatever you choose, exercise must be part of your healing journey and ongoing life, so start exploring your options. The thing is to *begin*. Just a walk around the block after dinner would be a great start.

Martial Arts

ACCORDING TO THE ENCYCLOPEDIA Britannica, there are at least 170 international martial arts. These are physical disciplines related to combat and self-defense. Martial alludes to Mars, the Roman god of war. The most well-known and popular martial arts are those from the Far East which are now widely followed across the world. They include judo, ju-jitsu, karate, taekwondo, and kendo. There are forms that are armed (using batons and swords) and those that are unarmed. Some such as tai chi are designated "internal martial arts," they are more concerned with self-defense and are practiced usually for their health benefits and as "moving meditations." Tai chi has become very popular, being recognized as a form of exercise accessible and beneficial to the elderly and others with physical limitations.

Martial arts usually have an associated philosophy. They require the practitioners to recognize and control aggression and focus their physical force. The discipline and self-mastery are very valuable for young people, who can begin to learn from as early as six years of age.

Highly skilled practitioners progress to working with weapons. There is always a philosophical and spiritual dimension, and very advanced students learn healing techniques as well.

The martial arts practices mentioned are widely taught in the west. In big cities, you may find classes on the lesser known types. The oldest martial art is reputedly Kalaripayattu, an Indian martial art mentioned in the 3000-year-old Hindu Vedas. Ninjitsu is a Japanese martial art believed to date from the 16th century, related to guerilla tactics and espionage and practiced by the so-called "ninja." I like to imagine myself flying through the trees as in the movie *Crouching Tiger, Hidden Dragon* as the ninja outfits are appealingly stylish, including the independently toed tarbi slippers, but realistically I should stick to my tai chi moves (Lee, 2000)!

Soul/Spirit

Yoga

YOGA MEANS UNION; FOSTERS the connection between mind, body, and spirit; and has mental and physical benefits. Again, there are now many forms of yoga to try. It is possible to practice yoga following online resources. They can never replace a good teacher, but if you have a full schedule or live somewhere remote from classes, it is another option.

Online taster sessions will give you an idea of the different styles and what would suit you. Hatha yoga is the kind we knew first in the west, building strength and flexibility and teaching relaxation. More intense and dynamic forms like ashtanga and vinyasa (flow) yoga are more energetic. Power yoga adds core and upper body work to standard hatha yoga asanas. Bikram yoga ("hot yoga") is delivered in a hot and steamy environment, encouraging sweating to release toxins. Iyengar yoga uses props like blocks and straps to facilitate highly precise positioning and long held poses. More gentle and relaxing versions of yoga include restorative yoga, where you relax into poses again using blocks and pillows and falling asleep is almost encouraged. Restorative yoga will have a focus on the "yoga nidra" relaxation component with guided meditations. Sivananda is another very relaxing form. There is special yoga practice for pregnancy, and even the theatricality of aerial and acro yoga for people who might like the upside-down poses, and in the case of acro yoga, working with a partner. There is also Kundalini yoga.

All yoga is great for maintaining flexibility, especially as we age or if we have a highly sedentary lifestyle with long hours in office chairs or the seats of vehicles. Different yoga practitioners will vary in how much they emphasize or verbalize the mental and spiritual aspects of the practice, but even a seemingly purely physical practice will affect the other areas, as they are designed to do.

Kundalini Yoga

I GAVE KUNDALINI YOGA practice its own little section here because it focuses on the fiery Kundalini energy. This *chi* or *prana* energy is visualized as a coiled serpent at the base of the spine. Kundalini yogic practice encourages this highly creative, sexual type of energy to awaken and rise up etheric channels in the spine, through the seven main *chakras* or energy centers. Adherents claim this type of yoga excels at helping you develop and express your unique creativity and at helping you live your most authentic and fulfilling life. Practitioners of Kundalini yoga traditionally wear white clothing, which they believe repels negativity. They use mantras. "Ong namo guru dev namo" (which could be translated as "I bow to the divine within myself.") introduces most Kundalini yoga sessions. There are chants and breath work, famously the "Breath of Fire" technique, sequences of poses and dynamic movements called *kriyas,* as well as meditative and relaxation practice.

Kundalini yoga is one of the more overtly spiritual yoga practices. It is brilliant for finding the real you, "coming home to yourself," and becoming the person you are meant to be. Practice Kundalini yoga, and the person you become can really surprise you.

Soul/Spirit

Magic

BY MAGIC, I AM SPEAKING of the traditional practices by which people seek to change their world by the action of their will. They use spells, rituals, and words to seek to influence things beyond their practical and physical power to control.

There are those who ridicule the notion of magic, as there is no explanation for how it might work. I believe, as did Shakespeare's *Hamlet* that: "there are more things in heaven and earth, Horatio, than are dreamt of in your philosophy" (Shakespeare, 1603). We do not know the mechanisms yet, but perhaps we will one day. In any event, we know the practice of magic is universal to all human cultures and times. Magic was often outlawed and proscribed. Why outlaw something if it is ineffective and nonsense? Probably because magic is about power, and there is a desire to restrict the exercise of power. Magic was ever the resort of those whose earthly power is restricted.

When magical practices are observed to produce results it is often posited that this results from the psychological effect of the deep belief of the practitioner. They create situations that fulfill the magic intention or achieve some sort of self-hypnosis that affects the situation. Certainly, they are right; magic depends on you *believing.*

Magic practices involve intention, focus, and ritual of some kind. Mental, emotional, and psychic energy is directed to the desired aim or object. Beyond that, I cannot explain the mechanism.

Being a form of power, magic can be misused and do harm, but the central tenet of ethical witchcraft (the practice of magic) is, "And it shall harm none, do what thou wilt." This has two important features. It expresses freedom and the exercise of free will, exhorts the practitioner to consider the effects and implications of their actions.

Consider if you wished to practice magic to enhance your chances of getting a job. It would not be ethical to cause harm or impediment to your rivals. You want rather for your abilities to be recognized (for example, being inspired to say the right things or express yourself well at your interview, not having your competitors knocked down by a bus.)

Magic especially belongs to fire in general because it is about power, action, and the exercise of personal will. However, all the elements have their magic expressions.

The particularly fiery forms of magic include practices involving candles, incense, censors (burners for oils and similar), lamps, and cauldrons.

Candle Magic

WORKING MAGIC WITH candles with magic is simple and popular. The color of the candle is significant and chosen for a particular purpose. White candles relate to calm, spirituality, and purity of intent. Yellow candles are high energy and intellectual; they will help with social connections and educational and work matters. Orange candles support changes and would be good for bringing new opportunities, like a new job. Green relates to growth and prosperity and enhances connection to nature. Pink is for love, affection, and kindness. Blue is for calm and good, clear communication. Red is for passion and sexual matters. Purple is for power and deep transformations. Black is the choice for invoking psychic protection.

When you have chosen your appropriate candle, it is dedicated and anointed, or dressed, to clarify and focus your intention. Rub with appropriate oils and decorate or carve to make your intention specific. Verbalize your intention and repeat or chant your wish as the candle burns. Perhaps for the new job scenario, you would choose an orange candle for change and new opportunities and a green one to attract prosperity. You might rub with a nice smelling oil like sweet almond for a harmonious working atmosphere. You might carve a word on the candle relating to the role or the company you want to join. You might speak a spell like, "And it shall harm none, let me gain this new job, if it supports the highest good and divine purpose of all concerned." As the candle burns, envisage yourself in the role and chant perhaps, "New opportunity, new prosperity and new success." Adding the bit about the "highest good" means that you will not get it if it is in fact not taking you on the best path forward in a way you cannot see as yet. If the company is not financially sound or is unethical or if a much better opportunity is just over the horizon, you will avoid a wrong move.

Obviously take care with candles and never leave them unattended.

Altars

ALTARS ARE SACRED SPACES that you can create in your personal and private space. They are a physical expression of your spiritual beliefs and intentions. An altar is a place for meaningful objects. Religious symbols and statues, such as statues of gods and goddesses and other beings that inspire you, belong on your altar. Talismanic objects and your spiritual tools, candles, crystals, incense, and prayers and inspiring words are brought together, and this creates a focal point for your devotional, spiritual, and magical practices. Ideally, they are in a peaceful place where you have the opportunity to retreat, reflect, and restore yourself. Altars need to be kept neat and clean, and updating them with fresh flowers or colors and objects that celebrate the season or your current projects reinforces the idea that you are connecting with spirit always and in all you do.

Ritual

RITUAL IS ANOTHER UNIVERSAL human practice. Weddings, bar mitzvahs, and birthday celebrations are all rituals. They are stylized expressions of important progressions and movements and achievements for individuals. When we carve pumpkins at Halloween or light firecrackers and attend lion dances at Chinese New Year or hang mistletoe at Christmas, we are participating in rituals that mark the turn of the seasons. Mexican culture has the Day of the Dead, with elaborate rituals celebrating rather than mourning the dead and symbolically inviting the ancestors to return and reconnect with the living.

Rituals demonstrate and affirm our intentions and spiritual beliefs. There is a belief across Europe that it is imperative for beekeepers to "tell the bees" when a death has occurred in the household. Sometimes hives are draped in sheets or scraps of black cloth. The bees then share in the mourning. There are superstitions that a failure to tell the bees will result in them swarming away, rejecting a new keeper if their keeper has died, or evil befalling the family. The ritual reflects the bond between people and bees, not just the gratitude of the beekeeper who harvests wax and honey, but the much more momentous human dependence on bees as pollinators of the crops that feed humanity.

Rituals can be group celebrations where we connect with others who share our interests and beliefs. We can connect with our tribe, be it our family or a "chosen family" of friends. Alternatively, rituals can be solitary. Rituals affirm, celebrate and focus attention on what really matters.

Important rituals are connected with death. Rites like funerals and traditions like wakes bring people together at a time of sadness and loss.

There are also small rituals of life, like closing curtains at night, winding clocks (I am sure some people still wind clocks), sweeping pathways, bedtime stories, and kissing children goodnight. They give us a sense of order and calm in the chaos of life. They are reassuring touchstones amid the challenges of each day. Lighting a small candle at our dinner table gives a sense of occasion to our evening meal. Celebrating and appreciating the coming together gives the time together a sense of the sacred, even if dinner is just beans on toast.

Think of the rituals in life and think about what they mean for you. How can you make them more special by some symbolic act? If you always enjoy a long leisurely bath on a Sunday, add a candle or a scented oil and celebrate the self-care and relaxation by giving your attention to the meaning.

The Fire Festivals

THE FIRE FESTIVALS were the eight ritually observed celebrations of the year. They celebrated the seasons and the cycle of sowing, growing, and harvesting crops. Observing the Fire Festivals can help city dwellers connect to nature and the seasonal round, as well as the wisdom of ancient lore. The Celtic year began with Samhain at the end of October. The Celtic druids or priests believed that the veils between the worlds of the living and the dead were at their thinnest at that time and it was possible to connect to the spirits of the dead. It was a dark, mysterious, and magical time. The Christian church incorporated this celebration into their calendar as The Feast of All Saints and All Souls. The celebrations featured hazelnuts and apples, and many Samhain rituals persist in today's Halloween celebration. In ancient days, the whole of November was dedicated to the cult of the dead as we all headed into the darkness and privations of winter.

Yule is celebrated at the Winter Solstice (Christian Christmastime) and celebrated the "return of the light." It involved celebrations and feasting and helped buoy spirits when days were dark and cold.

Imbolc, celebrated on February 1st, is a lovely festival, full of promise. It means "in the belly" and was the time when the lambs were growing but not yet born, when there are snowdrops and celandines, perhaps to show that winter will end, even if you cannot see it yet. The Church marked Imbolc as Candlemas and the feast day of St. Brigid. The next is the Spring Equinox festival called 'Eostre' after the Goddess of the Spring and the dawn. Christian Easter, a "moveable feast," is held the Sunday after the Full Moon after the Equinox. The celebrations still include the ancient ones of dyed eggs. Hot cross buns are like the spring cakes baked by the Romans and Greeks, and our Easter Bunny relates to the magical moon hare that represented the Goddess in pre-Christian times. In many Celtic countries, there is a taboo against the eating of hares, believed to be sacred animals. Sometimes witches transformed themselves into hares, it was believed. There was also a ritual once of putting out the household fires that had burned all winter, sweeping them out and laying them afresh.

Beltane is celebrated on May Eve, when the spring is in full swing. Lambs are skipping. Flowers, green branches, and blossoms are everywhere. Beltane celebrates fertility and sexuality, maypole dances, and May Kings and Queens, and "Green Men" ritually celebrate the fecundity of nature. May Eve was associated with fairies and was one of the times when it was believed you were most likely to see them or even be captured by fairies. Women dressed in green which in past times was thought to be particularly sexy, as red dresses are today. Originally red dresses and belts related to maternity and motherhood, green to maidens.

Midsummer marks the Summer Solstice, the longest day of the year, when crops are ripening in the fields. Midsummer "Baal fires" lit on hilltops were meant to banish evil and ensure a successful harvest. The associated Christian festival was St. John's Day, and rituals persisted like jumping over midsummer fires. It was a time of trysting, betrothals, and 'handfastings,' or weddings. Shakespeare's *A Midsummer Night's Dream* alludes to the mischievous fairy activity that took place at that time. They were believed to be attracted to the fires and liable to cause chaos. Sometimes people tied charms to the tails of cattle at Midsummer to protect them from fairies.

Lammas or Lughnasa in August marked the harvest. There were loaves baked with the first grain cut, threshed, and milled, and these were dedicated to the Goddess in thanks. Bounty was shared with the poor and needy.

The yearly festivals finish with the Autumn Equinox in late September. The tradition was to make a "corn dolly" of the final sheaves of the harvest and dress them to honor the Goddess. The year is now dropping towards the darkness of winter. It is a time of review and reflection, a time to make plans. Disputes had to be resolved and debts paid before the start of a new year at the next Samhain.

If the Celtic culture resonates or appeals to you, or perhaps is your ancestral heritage, you may enjoy marking these festivals. There are modern-day druids that meet and celebrate and honor the Goddess, or you can mark the festival by yourself. As well as linking to the cycles of the natural world, you can connect to the Goddess and thus the divine feminine within yourself. Imbolc, Eostre, and Beltane relate to the Goddess as the Maiden: Midsummer, Lammas, and the Autumn Equinox as the Mother; Samhain and Yule as the crone or older wise woman.

Chapter 4: Water: Riding the Waves, Going with the Flow

Water is about feeling and emotion. Water energy relates to the bonds of love and affection we feel for others and the care and kindness we show to express our love. Water connects us to the realms of the unconscious and the mysterious "universal unconscious." Springs feed streams that lead to lakes and rivers and seas and oceans. Water is beautiful and attractive. All life on earth originated in the oceans, and perhaps something in us remembers that. Water cleanses and refreshes, hydrates, and blesses. it is gentle and flowing, adaptable. It takes the form of whatever holds it, be it the basin of a lake or sea or a cup or chalice. It reflects visually. You can only see so far below the surface of the deep, beyond that is unfathomable mystery. But the water has extraordinary power, the power to wear away mountains or to rise in great waves and tsunamis or to wind into treacherous whirlpools. It is uncontainable, running through our fingers.

Mind

OH, THOSE PESKY EMOTIONS! If you have a high watery quotient in your make-up, life *is* emotion to you. It is how you understand life and process experience in a very conscious way. So often, we are brought up to control and suppress emotion, in a British "stiff upper lip" way. We are given the idea that expressing emotion is a sign of weakness and vulnerability, and that is just so wrong.

The sociology researcher Brene Brown became famous when she delivered one of the most viewed TED talks ever (Brown, 2011). She was interested in the characteristics of people who were living the most "whole-hearted," vibrant lives. She found that these people were courageous, compassionate, and connected well to people. They also were willing to share their vulnerability. This surprised her because she did not anticipate that strong and successful people would do that. It turned out that admitting failures and fears takes a lot of bravery and when you do it, you connect well with others because these are universal experiences. This creates situations where people feel they belong and fosters creativity and happiness.

Faced with difficult feelings like fear and shame, we often want to hide away or numb the feelings with various addictive and avoidant behaviors that do not serve us well. As Brown points out, when we block out negative feelings in this way, we are also blocking potential positive feelings like joy and gratitude.

Sharing or expressing difficult feelings take courage but also needs discrimination. There are environments and people where you will not meet an empathic and supportive response. It is not that you must be "wearing your heart on your sleeve" constantly. Pick carefully who you honor with the gift of your honest feelings, but do share them because only in this way can you live a really wholehearted, 'big' life. The best employers foster a work culture where employees feel safe to honestly share their experiences and ideas and indeed failures, knowing they will be met with support and appreciation. These are the sorts of places where people take risks and feel free and confident to be themselves and get creative and expressive; they are enjoyable as well as more productive.

How can you share more of your experience? Know that if you are "very emotional," this is a potential superpower. Your emotions are your hotline to what is really going on and what you need to know about yourself and others. Even negative feelings like envy, that we often feel we should reject or feel ashamed of, are really important information about what you really want and what you would be happier doing. Why does that person or place always fill you with dread? Trust your feelings. Analyze what it is that makes you feel that way and take the actions to address the difficulty, be it to confront and change something or to cut it out of your life.

Be a proud 'snowflake.' Sensitivity and vulnerability are *necessary* to true success.

Waiting on Your Wave

THAT IS THE OTHER THING about emotions. They take the time they take.

There is much better understanding today of emotional processes like grief, for example. If we are bereaved or suffer a significant loss of something in our lives, it is widely understood now that we typically go through a series of stages in coming to terms with the loss and there are various time frames involved.

If we are confronted with new information that we must absorb, watery emotional folks often need to give themselves time before reacting, responding, or especially before making important decisions. Let the new circumstance become part of you and wait until you feel ready to respond clearly. Learn to say, "Give me a day (an hour, 10 minutes) to think this through and I will get back to you." Wait on your emotional wave. Come back at it when you are steady, when you see it clearly, and when you can jump back in the flow elegantly.

Some people, instinctive more fiery types, and airy folk with supersonic logic skills, can respond or compute variables at lightning speed and act almost instantaneously. If that is not you, honor your energy. Watery types move at the speed of love, and that is variable.

I never accept a job offer in the moment. I would always say, "Thanks, I am so excited and happy you have asked me. However, I have a personal rule to always reflect carefully before big decisions. May I come back to you this afternoon (or tomorrow)?" I wait on my mental and emotional wave, and then I am confident about the new step and never rush into anything before my feelings have caught up.

The Magic Space Between Waking and Sleeping

THIS IS A STRANGE LIMINAL space and time. It is populated by the fleeting images of dreams and the first thoughts of the day. It is a time of special power, like the time when the Sun and the Moon are both visible in the sky. The conscious and the unconscious meet here.

It is also a time when we are highly impressionable, and we can use the power of this time if we pay attention to it. We can deliberately 'program' our minds with positive and uplifting intentions and use the images of dreams as keys to understanding ourselves. So we need to maximize the length of time we spend in the twilight states.

We can consciously ask our minds to find a solution to an issue concerning us while we sleep; not think about it, just set the intention of finding an answer and then leaving it for our wise unconscious to unravel. We can visualize how we want things to change. For instance, if we want to move somewhere new, we can picture ourselves in that new setting. Again, this is not the time for practical planning of your big move; just see yourself there. Similarly, when you wake, let yourself lie in the cozy warm, wake slowly, and introduce positive images of your ideal day. Harmonious and fun social interactions, effortless excellence and creativity at work, a relaxing dog walk, an inspiring visit to a theater or art gallery, or coffee with a good friend. Just set it up to flow beautifully. Include "good hair" and convenient parking spaces and public transport arriving at the perfect moment. Play and enjoy.

It works best if you avoid jarring and noisy alarms. At least start with a gentler version, the gently increasing chimes of a "zen alarm," a gentle alarm setting on your phone, or a special gentle waking alarm app. Then you are not torn brutally from the dream state but drift into your morning. If you are in bed early enough, you can set aside the time for this before the rush of breakfast and getting kids to school kicks in. It is like a spell or an "affirmation ritual." It is good for remembering dreams too.

Dreams

IF YOU DO NOT USUALLY remember dreams, you may find that using the sleep hygiene rituals and paying attention to the space between waking and sleeping helps you to start remembering them. Again, ask your mind to remember them on waking; it does work for some people. Sometimes you are aware of dreams at the time of waking, but by the time you reach the breakfast table they are long gone; if you are lucky, something that occurs during the day will spark a dream memory. People of my parents' generation would say, "Ah, that has broken a dream" when something brought back an image or a dream sequence. One trick is to keep a dream diary beside your bed. I have a special yellow exercise book and a matching yellow pencil. Unfortunately, sometimes I try to write when I am not quite enough awake, and the writing is illegible! The act of recording a dream diary is interesting, because as well as prompting you to remember more dreams, it will help you spot patterns and recurrent imagery.

You can do different things with dream imagery. You can analyze it in a very scientific or psychological way. The psychologist Carl Jung was fascinated by dreams and identified universal archetypes that pop up in dreams, such as figures of kings or princesses or dragons. You can also use them in a divinatory way and treat them as prophecies using various dream dictionaries. One of my favorites is *The Dreamer's Dictionary* (Robinson & Corbett, 1974/1987), although I own many, finding them interesting sources for understanding symbols in general. It can be extremely rewarding to use dream images and language to create art, stories, paintings, and, in my experience, especially sculpture. The process of turning the dream into the 'reality' of three dimensions can unlock the meaning or association.

Lucid dreaming is where you are dreaming but are aware this is a dream. This can happen spontaneously, or some people work to bring about lucid dreaming states so they can intentionally direct and rescript dreams. This has been useful for controlling and reducing the distress caused by recurrent nightmares.

You will find that dream work strengthens your intuition and your likelihood to engage with it in life. It is a psychic development tool.

Past Life Work

ANOTHER INTERESTING avenue to explore is the concept of past lives. For eastern cultures, it is part of religious and cultural belief that all does not end with death. Instead, the soul or spirit progresses to a new life experience. There is the idea that the soul evolves and improves through these experiences and the individual accrues positive or negative 'karma,' according to their conduct, that travels with them to the next life bank balance of virtue. Life experiences are not random but are attracted to us by our karma as we atone for our past mistakes and build up positive karmic capital.

There have been interesting investigations of small children remembering past lives in extraordinary detail that "check out" when historically investigated. The whole idea of reincarnation presents fascinating philosophical and ontological issues.

If you wish to explore past lives, then there are ways to access them. They can provide insight into unexplained issues, phobias, reactions, or attractions to people, places, or cultures that are otherwise unaccountable. You can work with psychologists that practice past life regression hypnosis where you personally experience episodes from one of your past lives. The episode that surfaces is the one with resonances and connections to your current life experience. There are some who believe that it does not matter if you 'believe' in reincarnation or not. If you don't, your regression 'recollections' are just stories your unconscious is telling you, which yield equally valuable insights. Past life therapists seek to help you understand and integrate the experiences and use past life experience to illuminate, explain, and heal current scenarios.

It is also possible to consult intuitive past life readers who can access this information for you psychically; typically, they will visit several past life scenarios.

Often the past life experience is a trauma, where you carry the imprint of the trauma into this life. For instance, if you are attacked by wolves in a past life, you may carry into this life an inexplicable fear of dogs despite no negative experience to explain it. Lots of people travel and suddenly experience a powerful and emotional response to a new location; they have 'been there before. It feels like coming home and, very possibly, they are.

Body

Sleep

WE SPEND A HUGE PART of life asleep, and this is because it serves really important functions. As well as giving your body a chance to rest and carry out maintenance like muscle repair, sleep is vital to our brains in processing information and experiences. It affects our emotions (as well as other things) by allowing endocrine levels to come into optimal balance.

It has been scientifically demonstrated that poor sleep contributes to the development of depression, diabetes, decreased strength and energy levels, immune system problems, obesity, and other illnesses. Poor sleep has a negative impact on our social interactions and our cognitive abilities and concentration.

The actual amount of sleep we need depends on age and varies between individuals. But we all need to maximize the quality of sleep we get. There is an art to optimal sleep; it is called "sleep hygiene."

First consider your sleeping space. Keep it as tidy and clutter-free as possible. Ideally a bedroom is a bedroom and not used for any other function. Setting up a home office in your bedroom is a bad idea if you have any other option; find somewhere else to be your sewing station or exercise space. Dedicate the room to sleep. Soft lighting and relaxing colors like blue and green are good for creating a restful atmosphere. Invest in the best and comfiest bed, pillows, and linens you can afford. A mattress that adequately supports your back is important.

Then add in a routine that helps you glide into optimal, restorative sleep. One of the enemies of sleep are our ubiquitous screens. If you cannot eliminate screens in the two hours before you sleep, at least dim the brightness of the screens. Ban yourself from watching any media in bed. If you want to do that, get up and move to the sofa, remembering the bedroom is for sleeping. For some reason, reading is not so bad. A book at bedtime is conducive to good sleep, maybe not horror stories though.

It is also good to avoid eating in the two hours before going to sleep; it is not just cheese that disturbs your dreams. If you have a problem relaxing, you might try a gentle herb tea, like chamomile, or lime flowers, or passion flowers. Stimulants should be avoided, ideally from midafternoon, for obvious reasons. Some people respond to herbal pillows stuffed with lavender or from scented "pillow sprays." An evening stroll or a warm bath can be a brilliant wind-down. Do not expect to go from high-octane activity to adequately restful sleep at a snap of the fingers.

Your sleep hygiene routine and environment can be a brilliant and easily instituted part of a coping mechanism for a stressful life, and falling into bed should be a blissful anticipation, not a collapse.

Swimming

SWIMMING IS BRILLIANT physical exercise. It has cardiovascular health and muscle strengthening effects. The water helps to support the body, and this is useful in reducing impacts on compromised joints. It is rhythmic and relaxing and can be almost meditative, or you can smash into an energetic front crawl and race against yourself and others. I personally manage a slow breaststroke with my nose in the air like an otter as I have never mastered proper technique, but I can swim forever and absolutely adore it.

There is an increasing interest in "wild swimming." If you are lucky enough to live by a lake, river, or sea where this is possible, it has great healing potential. You need to assess the safety of the swimming situation. Never wild swim alone; assess the suitability of the water. Consider tides, currents, wildlife, pollution levels, roughness, and, importantly, temperature because cold water shock is a killer. In some situations, a wetsuit is advisable. Curious seals have been known to playfully nip, except they have big teeth and poor dental hygiene so their bites can cause considerable damage.

If there is a suitable opportunity, wild swimming adherents enthuse about the benefits. It is energizing and exhilarating and connects you to nature. It has been shown to have a wonderful effect in reducing depression and strengthening immunity. Studies showed that regular wild swimming significantly reduced the number of colds people caught. Where I live, a group of "women of a certain age" meet daily and call their club "The Menopausal Mermaids." They swim in the North Atlantic daily, storms permitting.

In a city you may be able to visit an outdoor pool, perhaps one of the beautiful 'lidos' surviving from the 30s or 50s. I once lived near a pool with an ingenious indoor/outdoor arrangement. You jumped in under the shelter of the building into a warm area and swam out to the garden space where leaves settled on the water or, blissfully, rain pattered around you as you swam.

In any case, as the lifeguards tell us, always respect the water and make sure you are safe where you swim.

Water Within

WE ARE TOLD OUR BODIES are 80 percent water, sometimes more. Maintaining adequate hydration is vital to health. Humans survive a long time without food, but not long without water. Health experts tell us we need to drink eight glasses of water a day, or perhaps a minimum of one and a half liters. In our busy lives, it is easy to neglect this, and it has dire consequences for our health and well-being. Summer heat and exercise further deplete levels.

Every system of our body needs adequate hydration. Getting enough water can boost cognitive functioning. Not enough people realize the magic effect of drinking sufficient water on efforts to lose weight. Water flushes toxins from our body. It helps you maintain clear skin and bright eyes. In fact, it is the world's best, and incidentally cheapest, beauty product.

It is easy to slake our thirst with stimulants like tea and coffee, which are ultimately dehydrating to our bodies. Try to remember to match your caffeinated beverages with glasses of water. The quality of the water is worth considering too. If your municipality water treatment uses agents you want to avoid, perhaps chlorine and fluorine and such, you may want to filter your drinking water. Mineral and spa waters can taste lovely, but plastic bottle waste and air miles are climate change and conservation concerns. If you want to buy bottled water, choose glass bottles and the most local source. Water filters, from simple jug filters to more sophisticated systems attached to your water supply and taps, are other options. Try to carry a reusable water bottle with you always. I worked in an office that instituted an office-wide water challenge, and we all had charts on our desk to record the glasses of water drunk during the day. We installed a water dispenser supplied by a delicious regional mineral water source. It was part of their investment in their employees' health, and they knew it boosted productivity.

Healing Water

AN UNDERSTANDING OF the healing power of water is ancient and worldwide.

There are famous spas, like those at Baden Baden in Germany or Bath or Malvern or Glastonbury in the UK, where people once flocked to drink the restorative and therapeutic waters, and their popularity created thriving resorts. There are miraculous healing springs like the one at Lourdes in France. In Ireland there are numerous "holy wells," some with a recognized power for curing certain types of complaint.

Sometimes the cures are explained as the effect of the patient's fervent belief. The Catholic church has rigorous criteria for the assessment of true miracles at sites such as Lourdes, and this status is only rarely granted.

The effect of these waters cannot often not be demonstrated or explained scientifically, beyond having a desirable balance of minerals which would not seem enough to reverse a serious illness. The work of Masaru Emoto in *The Hidden Messages in Water* claimed to show differences in the crystalline structure of water in microscopic photographs (Emoto, 2001). Healing waters like Lourdes water, holy water, or water exposed to loving and kind messages showed exquisite symmetry and beauty. The photographs of highly polluted or irradiated water and water exposed to messages of hate or violence appeared disordered and chaotic. Emoto's work is roundly condemned by the scientific establishment as pseudoscience which is inadequately researched, reviewed, and tested. It is such a beautiful idea, and the images are so very compelling that I am loath to dismiss it. It was a bestseller when it came out, so clearly it had an appeal. Perhaps we should think of it as a metaphor for the mysterious healing powers of water.

No one can explain or argue with the soothing effects of spending time next to water, watching the ocean tides ebb and flow, the energetic course of a mountain stream or waterfall, or the stately progress of a majestic river. If fate distances you from these, you can install a water fountain in your living room or share your life with some beautiful pet fish.

Bath

WHAT CAN I SAY? WARM water, bubbles perhaps; the gift of an hour to rest and relax and ease tired muscles; the ceremony of a scented candle; a favorite book with pages swollen by the steam; the childish humor of a bobbing rubber ducky. A bath is one of life's simple pleasures, irrefutably healing.

Soul/Spirit

Meditation

MEDITATION IS THE NAME of various practices that aim to still the mind, create calmness, and facilitate spiritual and personal insight. Many cultures and most spiritual traditions embrace a form of meditation. Sometimes it is hard to untangle the effects and aims of a meditation practice from the religious or spiritual tradition that developed it.

It is popular now to practice meditation in a secular way, with an aim of reducing stress and anxiety, increasing insight, and promoting personal development.

Often the practice is to sit in a particular pose, focus the attention on an object, and dismiss any thoughts that intrude or come to mind. Focus on the breath is common or focus on an object like a candle flame, a flower, sounds, and repeated words or phrases (mantras). When the mind is divested of extraneous or random or obsessive thoughts, the mind is freed for spontaneous realizations about the self or the nature of things to be able to arise. Many find the practice to be calming and centering.

There are moving meditations too. The Vietnamese spiritual teacher Thich Nhat Hanh described this in his book *Peace in Every Step*. Some practitioners of tai chi consider their holistic moving martial art practice to be a moving meditation.

Some practices include repeated prayers and chants and 'mantras.' The Krishna Consciousness Movement is famous for its joyous mantra "Hare Krishna, Hare Rama." In the Roman Catholic church, religious litanies are repeated, and the repetitive prayers of the rosary are said, counting the number of repetitions on rosary beads.

It takes practice to still the mind and develop a truly contemplative practice, but benefits are derived from even a few minutes of regular practice. Scientific research has shown that real physiologically beneficial changes occur with extensive meditation practice, with alterations in levels of, for example, the stress hormone cortisol, and even physical changes in brain structure.

It is a personal choice whether your meditation is tied to a religious or spiritual practice or is practiced purely for personal development and wellbeing. Many people find communal practice helps them develop their personal practice and is a way to learn techniques. A session of meditation, however short, allows you to come back to the world refreshed, calmer and more focused. Sometimes people designate a daily period of 'sitting' with aspects of meditation, prayer, and spiritual healing practices. Giving yourself that quiet time is a strong commitment to self-care.

The mind has a natural inclination to wander. Inevitably that happens, especially when you first practice meditation. The response is simply to notice that you have drifted back to thinking and calmly bring your attention back to your chosen focus. Meditation teachers liken these unruly thoughts to clouds in the sky. You can notice them, not react, and allow them to drift away. When your mind is still, it is like the cloudless sky.

Quakers have a religious practice of sitting in silence, which they do not characterize as meditation. They say their silent worship is more passive, they do not actively focus on anything, but passively allow the running narrative of thoughts in their mind to simply fall away. They believe this creates a space for the Holy Spirit to inspire them, and if this occurs, they may be moved to speak.

If the idea of meditation appeals, you will be able to find many meditation groups and try different styles and approaches until you find something that works for you.

It is great to allow yourself time for meditation before an important event, meeting, interview, or session with a client, so you are calm, focused, and fully present and able to give your best to any situation.

Some meditators express an aim to extend their practice so eventually all their lives are an ongoing meditation. This might be easier for monastics in an environment of quiet, concentrated spirituality than in most people's busy lives! However it fits into your life, however small and simple or intense and complex your practice, repetition will develop mental and spiritual 'muscles' so that, whenever it is most needed, you can bring yourself to a state of calm centeredness.

Power of Myth and Story

DO YOU ENJOY STORIES? Someone once told me that there is a story-shaped hole in the human brain, developed since the time our earliest ancestors sat around fires and told stories. Every tale of what had happened carried vital information that could help you survive. Now we tell stories in many ways, with films and videos and books and podcasts and songs. We delight in the expression of something we have felt and wondered if it was only us that ever thought that, feeling less lonely, understood, and validated. Stories thrilled us with the tales of heroes who inspire us and models to follow in our own lives. Stories convey to us the values of our tribe, community, or society and help us develop our own moral compass.

Stories like *Harry Potter, EastEnders* episodes, and blockbuster and cult films are facets of our modern mythology, but we still tell and retell the old stories, the ancient myths, and sagas. The earliest stories we hear are often fairy tales. These stories are central to our understanding of life because they deal in archetypes and primal human experiences. Versions of Cinderella are told the world over. Some fairy tales are very dark and frightening, and yet we still tell them to children and children love them. In the fairy story, they first meet the monsters and the ogres and the wicked stepmothers and wolves and the dark lonely woods that they will encounter in some guise later in life.

Bruno Bettelheim explored the function of fairy tales in his psychoanalytic treatise *The Uses of Enchantment* (Bettelheim, 1976).

For women, Clarissa Pinkola Estes' work *Women Who Run with the Wolves* is a Jungian interpretation of fairy tales and folk tales from around the world that relate to the experience of women (Pinkola Estes, 1992). It is exciting, for it shows how we are distanced from our true self-expression, essential nature, and creativity, and inspires us to reconnect to the vital and vibrant wild self.

Most people remember a particular fairy tale, the one they wanted to be told over and over. There is something in that story that relates to a core issue or fear or desire that is particularly important to us. Surprisingly often, people find that in some sense, they have recreated aspects of their favorite fairy tale in their own lives. If it was Hansel and Gretel, a person might have a greater than normal fear of abandonment and either protect themselves or attract that experience in their lives. They are armed with the knowledge that even if that happens, they can use their wits to survive in forests, prevail over murderous witches, and by careful planning and foresight (leaving trails of crumbs), they can find their way home (to self-understanding, self-reliance and self-acceptance). Snow White and Little Red Riding Hood speak to the fears around adult sexuality particularly. The Celtic myth of the selkie reflects the female responsibilities of child-rearing and nurturing and devotion to family. While so valued and enriching, these often require a woman to lay aside her wild, self-expressive (seal) nature. She must shed that wild self, the way the selkie sheds her seal skin to become the devoted and beautiful wife and mother. When the selkie later finds her hidden and almost forgotten seal skin ("soul skin," as Estes calls it) later in life, she will not be able to resist jumping back into it and reclaiming her wild nature or true self.

You can apply this analysis of story to any favorite book or film that you return to again and again, typically the "comfort movie" or novel you reread year after year. What is it in that story that is calling you back to your true, authentic self?

Stories are entertaining and escapist, but they can also be precious clues to our "true self" and deepest desires and motivations. They are keys to self-knowledge and signposts to healing.

Tuning into the Cycles of the Moon

ONE OF THE MOST POWERFUL healing things a woman can do is to mark and notice the cycles of the Moon, from new waxing to Full and then waning back to dark and emerging new again.

Consider how the Moon's orbit moves huge bodies of water in the earth's oceans and seas and creates the tides. Consider how our bodies are at least 80 percent water. We know our menstrual cycles mirror the cycles of the Moon. Honoring and marking the phases of the Moon is honoring the cycles and tides within us. It is like falling into step with your body and emotions.

The phases of the Moon each have their own character and emphasis. The dark of the Moon is a time of withdrawal and inward reflection. It is a time for 'pathworking' (ritual meditations to connect to spirit guides and inner wisdom) and magic. A day or so later, the tiny sliver of the new Moon appears. This is the time to set new intentions for the month as inspired by your dark of the Moon meditations. Write them down or create ceremonies to commit to your goals. By the first quarter, you will be aware of the challenges and adjustments you might need to make in this endeavor. At the full Moon, you can assess your work. What have you achieved or what have you learned? How will you express it and celebrate it? By the third, waning quarter of the moon, you will be adjusting and completing your monthly process and getting ready for a new cycle.

Wiccans and neo-pagans follow the Moon in their worship of the Goddess, the deification of the feminine principle. Honoring the Goddess mirrors honoring the feminine within. They call on the Goddess to support their intentions, and their achievements and creations every Moon cycle are gifts back to her.

You can follow how your menstrual cycle corresponds to the Moon cycle. Notice and respect the waxing and waning of energies and emotions that reflect the cycles. Your menstrual cycle is your internal tidal system, and it is powerful. As much as you can, adjust your schedule to fit your activities to how you expect to feel. Of course, life doesn't always allow us to do that completely, but we can accommodate our cycle to the extent we are able.

A more sophisticated and especially useful practice is to follow the passage of the Moon around the zodiac. As it passes from sign to sign every two to three days or so, if you are attuned, you will notice a change in the energy of the world. When the Moon is in Gemini, people are chatty and busy and thirsty for gossip and knowledge. When the Moon is in Cancer, they are sensitive, touchy, moody, and emotional; when it is in Virgo, they are hardworking, analytical, critical, and discriminating. You will not notice this in every individual, but if your work brings you into contact with the public or you are out in crowds, you will see and feel that when the Moon changes sign, the atmosphere in a room shifts. Consult an astrologer to learn how every sign corresponds to a different horoscope 'house' on your astrological chart and what area of life that relates to for you. When the Moon is in your fifth house, it is the time to play, flirt, socialize, and create; when the Moon is in the sixth house, it is the time to get down to work, take care of details, and dot your i's and cross your t's. When the Moon is in the ninth, go somewhere different, seek out a new experience, learn something, or connect to the divine, whatever that means to you. In the fourth, enjoy being with your family or at home, snug and safe and domestic. An astrologer can talk you through the 12 signs for you and then, if you emphasize the activities the Moon is illuminating, you will have a tailwind behind those activities.

Following the Moon connects you with the heavens: "As Above, So Below." The stars and the planets have wisdom and guidance worth exploring.

Divination

DIVINATION IS THE NAME given collectively to magical practices that reveal to us unseen realities. Divination gives us glimpses of the future and gives us insight into the hidden motivations of others or into the value or potential of projects or intentions that are not clear to us. Divinatory practices employ tools or rituals focusing intuition to help us make decisions when we cannot have sufficient information to make rational assessments or when we are confused or conflicted. Using symbolic systems like tarot and runes, casting the coins or yarrow sticks for an I Ching reading, or using other similar oracles is divination.

Some systems yield explicit answers; others are more nuanced and require the reading of symbols and the use of intuition. The more you use these tools, the sharper your intuition becomes. Even an experienced and insightful reader of cards or tea leaves or rune stones cannot really be objective when reading for themselves; one's preconceptions and wishful thinking or fears creep into the reading. It is better to find a reader but be careful to find someone ethical and compassionate; seek recommendations.

Divination can be illuminating, but do not let it become addictive. Perhaps incorporate divination into your scheduled Moon rituals or reserve it for times when it is really needed. If you are frivolous and repetitive in your demands for answers, 'Spirit,' the magic force behind the divination, will not serve you.

Astrology is rather different, being both an art and a science; intuition is employed in readings, but there is a vast aspect of precise symbolism and mathematical measurement and timings that is craft rather than magic. There is a special branch of astrology called horary that is essentially divinatory, although it is read from an astrological chart. Horary answers very specific questions. Interpreted by an accomplished astrologer, horary is spookily accurate.

Dowsing is a simple do-it-yourself divination method. You focus on your question and see the response of a swinging crystal pendulum or dowsing rod. Simple, but not always easy. It seems dowsing talent is not universal, but most people can develop some degree of ability.

If you are magically inclined, divinatory practices are fascinating to explore. All of them develop your extrasensory perceptive powers, be they clairvoyant, clairaudient, olfactory, or sentient. Protect yourself psychically when you practice, with protective crystals and shielding, as necessary. Cover yourself with light and invoke the protection of angels and ancestors and the higher spiritual beings that most appeal to you before you work. Commit yourself to the highest healing intentions and moral standards.

Vision Boards

VISION BOARDS ARE A fun and creative way to use imagery to set and commit to intentions to change and heal yourself and bring your life into alignment with your highest purpose and true self. If you are not clear what that looks like, the vision board process can help you clarify. It is a delightfully playful exercise of cutting and sticking that will have you happily in touch with your nursery school inner child.

One method is to flick through piles of old magazines and cut out all the images that appeal to you, without too much analysis. Arrange them aesthetically on your board. Then consider what it is that drew you to that image. A picture of an idyllic natural scene could be a yearning for peace and connection to the natural world. A fairy tale cottage could speak of a need for security or a settled home. Toys or images of children could speak of your need for play and fun and creativity or perhaps your longing to have a child. A fast car could relate to your need for power and control or a desire for excitement. Are there colors that dominate in your choices? What do those colors symbolize for you?

If your images all seem to relate to a specific area of life, you can choose to keep that focus and search for more images about love, work, family, health, spirituality, security, or whatever it is. Or you can look for images that speak about other areas of life, so your vision board reflects everything, relationships and creativity and connection to the divine and all the main areas that matter to you. Have fun sticking down the image and arranging them. You can order them to create a balanced visual composition, order them according to the main priority, or group together connected ideas.

If you do feel you have a clear vision of the future, you can seek out imagery and even make drawings to create a collage of those specific elements you wish to "call in to manifestation." What this process lacks, however, is the surprise element of 'found' imagery and the learning that comes from letting yourself choose instinctively and only afterwards asking what it means. Doing it spontaneously gets your mind out of the way and lets your subconscious guide you with its deeper wisdom.

Put your finished vision board somewhere you will see it daily, and let the imagery go to work on your subconscious. Make a new one every year or so. When moving to a new house, I discovered some old vision beards created a decade before. It was interesting to see how many of the dream images had become real. Other pictures made me smile because those things had lost their significance or importance.

Success and healing start with intention. A vision board is a statement of intent; keep that in mind as you make it. If you are a watery person particularly, your mind is likely to be quite visual, and images will speak to you. Making vision boards is very playful and incredibly fun.

Chapter 5: Air: Only Connect

The element of air has a cool, fast-moving, and detached quality. It is intellectually and mentally focused. Air is the realm of ideas and theories, of communication and connection. Air likes to make links between ideas and links between people and ideas. Air is interested in relationships. It always wants to know something new and find someone to share the new thing with and something innovative to do with it.

Mind

Knowing the Self

THE CHINESE PHILOSOPHER and sage Lao Tzu who was believed to have lived in the 6th century BC said, "Knowing others is wisdom, knowing yourself is enlightenment." Many Greek philosophers cited the maxim "know thyself," and apparently it was carved on a temple in the ancient sanctuary of Delphi.

We get subsumed into hectic lives and sometimes fail to spend the time to explore and consider who we really are. How can you make the right decisions and choices in life if you are unclear about what you want and what matters to you? Sometimes crises in life, whether mental, physical, or emotional, bring us to a halt to create the space to "know ourselves."

Depression can be viewed as part of a process of alignment, a dark, dissolved, confusing chrysalis state that we need to get through in order to emerge transformed into who or what we are meant to be. You can get the help, therapy or medication you need to respond properly to a serious and disabling depression and at the same time hold the thought that it is a 'process' that has meaning and will lead back to the light.

Therapy that explores your personal psychological make-up can be very enlightening. While you are addressing specific issues, you will learn a lot about yourself. Therapies are not just about fixing a specific problem, ideally it is about personal development. Eric Berne's transactional analysis was a psychological movement that explored what we can learn about ourselves by looking at our interactions with others. Person-centered therapy, introduced by Carl Rogers, aimed to help people change themselves and their lives to express their true individual nature and authentic selves in a process called 'self-actualization.' Jeffrey Young's schema therapy explores the maladaptive habitual thought systems we have, often subconscious, that are blocking our development. These are just some of many psychological theories that can be explored in our quest to know ourselves better.

If you do not want or need to dive into a full therapeutic experience, there are interesting 'psychometric' tests available online that can give interesting insights.

One very established test is the Myers-Briggs test. It measures by a long series of questions the balance of certain personal dynamics first outlined by Jung as fundamental orientations to life. It shows whether you are more introverted or extroverted, more inclined to use intuition or senses in apprehending the world, more a thinking or a feeling person in the way you respond to the world, and whether you are more 'perceiving' or 'judging,' i.e. more likely to be flexible in your reactions to things or liable to stick to a fixed response. The test identifies sixteen "personality types," e.g. INFJ (the introverted, intuitive, feeling, and judging combination). It is frequently used in recruitment procedures to determine a person's suitability for a role. However, the ramifications of each personality type go far beyond their work experience and are illuminating to explore.

Another classic psychometric test is the Belbin team roles test, again beloved of the folks in Human Resources. The questions measure certain traits that fit you for roles within organizations. Some people are suited to leadership, others for coming up with ideas, networking, checking details and processes, encouraging, and supporting others, or bringing teams together. Not everyone is supposed to be a "team player." All the roles are valuable and necessary and being clear about your key strengths helps you pick work roles where you will be a round peg in a round hole.

Socrates taught that "an unexamined life is not worth living." He meant that only by thinking about ourselves and our experiences do we understand our personal values and the meaning of our lives. Viktor Frankl survived the Holocaust in a concentration camp. He attributes his survival to his intense focus on his personal values and clear understanding of the meaning of his life and ability to imagine a future when those true values are expressed that enabled him to transcend the unimaginable horror of his environment. His story is recounted in *Man's Search for Meaning* (Frankl, 1946/1959). He went on to dedicate his life to psychotherapy, helping others find meaning. We can survive almost anything if we know why.

Journaling and Writing

JOURNALING AND WRITING are great ways to get to know yourself. *Writing Down the Bones* is a classic book that has great suggestions for "freeing the writer within" (Goldberg, 1986/2005). It is full of tricks for quieting the internal critic that stifles real self-expression. Airy folk often love to write and sometimes have the odd experience of only knowing something about how they felt when reading what they have written down. Certainly, a journal is an accessible private space to record thoughts and experiences, and entails reflection and some analysis. A character in one of Oscar Wilde's plays said, "I never travel without my diary, one should always have something sensational to read on the train," (Wilde, 1895) and no one is sure which wit first said: "Keep a diary and one day it will keep you," inferring that your memoirs could eventually be bestsellers, and who knows?

Creative writing classes abound, with "life writing" a great favorite. The great crime writer P.D. James said, "All fiction is largely autobiographical, and much autobiography is, of course, fiction." It doesn't matter; even if the facts are "adjusted," the deeper truth and the reality of a feeling or an experience tends to be unmistakable to readers and listeners. Or, as Mark Twain is believed to have said: "Never let the truth get in the way of a good story."

Writing is a powerful tool for understanding the self. It is a place to explore, express, and process difficult emotions and experiences, and many have found their diaries and journals great friends and sources of solace in difficult times. Buy a nice notebook for your journal and a pen you like to demonstrate the value of the investment in yourself that is writing.

Every Day Is a School Day

IF YOU DID NOT HAVE the most positive experience of school, this heading can seem a little unappealing. I am not necessarily talking about any formal educational experience. It is a fundamental pillar of wellbeing to keep learning. The human brain is wired for it.

It could be as simple as seeking out books and TV shows on a topic that fascinates you. Perhaps you love to learn about the Jazz Age or Arctic wildlife or the history of your home village. Perhaps you want to try something hands on like printing, découpage, or silversmithing. Adult education facilities are the places to "have a go" at new things and meet others who share your enthusiasm.

Ideally your work life should be full of learning and self-development, but not everyone is lucky enough to find themselves in a fulfilling role. Learning things outside work may be the first step to transitioning into work that will inspire you and that you will enjoy. This could be where a hobby morphs into a new career where you find yourself in the enviable situation of doing what you love as a job.

Learning does not have to be something so formal. You might enjoy relaxing by reading. Fiction is not just a whodunit or romance or family saga; it creates a world in the imagination. As an aside, you learn about medieval France, or the esoteric world of advertising, or nurses in the first world war. Learning a new language always involves absorbing something of the culture to which it belongs. You can have fun in a conversational class, practicing phrases to use on a special holiday trip, or learn Russian so you can read Dostoevsky in the original. You can learn to repair your own motorcycle or grow vegetables or keep tropical fish.

If you have been having a hard time, being ill or unhappy, it is easy to disconnect from the things in life that foster wellbeing. Learning is one of them. Start in a small way if that is what you can manage but try to build it into your life.

Handwriting

HERE IS A STRANGE THING I learned recently. Graphology is the art of handwriting analysis. You can look at the shape of letters and the slant of the writing, the relative heights of letters and even the way the writing is arranged on a page and discover things about the writer's personality. It could go in the "Know Thyself" section above, except that what was interesting was that apparently it is possible to effect personal change by deliberately altering your handwriting (Rogers, 2000). Making taller f's or eliminating certain loops or extraneous backwards ticks can have an impact on your behavior and experience. It is certainly a surprising idea but is not at all a new idea. There are ancient Kabbalistic texts that allude to the same idea and the necessity of forming letters with great care.

For instance, filling pages completely and not leaving any margins, suggests someone is subconsciously not leaving space for others in their life. Deliberately leaving adequate margins could encourage more connections, friendships, and partners, and so on.

Astrology

ASTROLOGY IS AN EXTRAORDINARILY complex art which reads the mysterious correspondences between the movements of stars and planets in the solar systems and the things that happen on earth. Mundane astrology examines world events and politics. Personal astrology uses the information of a person's time, date, and place of birth to construct a "natal chart," which is a celestial map for the precise moment of a person's birth. This can be interpreted as a complex blueprint for the life potentials of the individual. It indicates their personality traits, likely life experiences and challenges, talents, and weaknesses. It is not a totally fatalistic system; the chart in fact distinguishes what are likely to be the proclivities and free will intentions of the person and how these are likely to clash or coincide with "fate."

Astrology is not what we all enjoy as "sun sign" astrology columns in the newspapers, which are an absurd oversimplification of a highly sophisticated art. Astrology is a symbolic language which has been practiced at least since Babylonian times. There are many schools of astrology and different types of astrological practice.

Astrology is certainly a brilliant tool for self-knowledge and self-development. There are endless resources online these days, including free tutorials to begin to understand your chart. Nothing will replace the experience of a reading from a competent, trained astrologer.

There are modern psychologically oriented schools of astrology. Important writers in this field are Liz Greene and the late Howard Sasportas. Evolutionary astrologers focus on the "soul purpose" of a person's life and experience. Traditional astrologers used ancient techniques and are strong on prediction and timings. Horary is a divinatory branch of astrology with its own arcane rules that uses astrological techniques to answer extremely specific questions. Most successful professional astrologers will be practiced in all these techniques but will have a preferred orientation.

Choose a practitioner that is affiliated and recommended by a professional body, such as the Association of Professional Astrologers or the Astrological Association in the UK or the delightfully named C*I*A (Cosmic Intelligence Agency), which has numbered 'agents' who are a broad range of competent international practitioners. Be clear what you are looking for. Do you want psychological insights, are you wanting specific predictions or timings, or are you more focused on your "soul path"? Good astrologers' study for many years (in fact they never stop learning) and preparation takes time, so astrology is not cheap. With some effort you will find the right astrologer for you.

If you want to do it yourself, great beginners' books are *The Inner Sky* by Steven Forrest and the hilarious classic *Secrets From a Stargazer's Notebook* by Debbie Kempton Smith.

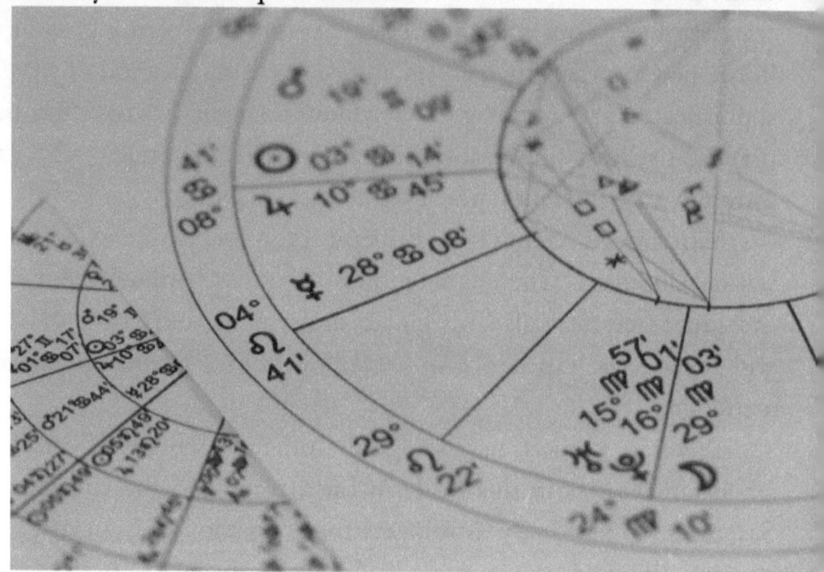

Gratitude

AN INTERESTING AND unexpectedly effective healing technique is keeping a gratitude journal. This is the practice of daily making a note of all the good things you have done or seen or experienced in a day. When life is grim and tough, this technique really comes into its own. Even if your world is falling apart and you are coping with the hard things that come to us all at some point, you carefully note every little thing that lifts your spirit.

"There was a goldfinch on the bird feeder this morning. Someone at work said I was always great at coming up with ideas. I did a perfect parallel park, first try, outside the grocery store. My favorite pasta sauce was on sale. My little boy's laugh fills me with warmth and joy. I love riding my bicycle, it is so good that there are lots of cycle paths around here. I love how my cat rushes to greet me when I get home for work." Give it a go, it does make you feel better.

It is just training your mind to "accentuate the positive" and put a positive spin on things. The human mind is wired to emphasize the negative. It is the caveman mind that needed to pay more attention to the saber-tooth tiger than the flowers. You do not need help being aware of what is going wrong. It is about connecting to the little rays of light that will help you keep going through the dark times.

Body

Macrobiotics

MACROBIOTICS WILL APPEAL to the airy mind because it has a lot of theory and philosophy behind it. It is a complicated but truly holistic approach to health. A macrobiotic lifestyle is endorsed by celebrities like Madonna, Gwyneth Paltrow, and Alicia Silverman. Madonna attributed the macrobiotic diet with giving her the stamina to perform to her highest standard during long, grueling international tours.

The founder of macrobiotics is George Ohsawa. He became interested in health and nutrition after tuberculosis claimed most of his close family. Mishio Kachi brought macrobiotics to the western world.

Diet is central to macrobiotics, a particular diet modeled on the diets worldwide that seem to result in the longest and healthiest lives, free of chronic illnesses. However, it is much more than that. 'Macro-bio' means big life and it is about having the most vibrant and fulfilling life experience, not just beautiful skin, shiny eyes, and a lithe slinky body. Macrobiotic people are typically into forms of holistic movement, yoga or tai chi or five-rhythms dance. They are committed and enthusiastic lifelong learners and do not compromise about lifestyle or the job they do.

The diet is usually but not exclusively plant based. In fact, it is not stringent about what is included. It recognizes that the needs of an athlete competing in Iron Man are different from those of a painter in oils. Men and women and children all have different requirements. The core of the diet is always whole grains, with special emphasis on brown rice. It is carbohydrate rich. Fresh vegetables are important too. Tofu, tempeh, and plant-based proteins feature. Dairy products and certain other foods are not part of the plan. Some vegetables are discouraged, notably the wicked members of what they call the "nightshade family":

tomatoes and peppers and potatoes. Tomatoes are way too acidic. Potatoes might be allowed if you live in the high Andes where they originate, when your body and its interaction with the high-altitude environment make you and potatoes adapted to each other. Peppers in moderation might be ok if you live in sunny southern Europe; if you live in Queen's or Tottenham, you have no business chowing down on them in quantity. Things are always ok as treats or in moderation. Sea vegetables feature quite prominently and fermented foods too. Sushi is cute and trendy macrobiotic fare (it doesn't have to have fish in it), and if you get into this, you will soon own a sushi mat and have nori sheets in your cupboard.

The fitness of foods for your sex, age, activity, and constitution is determined by the yin-ness or yang-ness of things. You are always seeking to achieve an energetic balance of yin and yang. Red meat, for instance, is super 'yang,' and beyond unbalancing your body can provoke too much aggressive single focus. Alcohol and refined sugar are too super 'yin' and can make you scattered, overly emotional and lacking in direction. Brown rice and miso soup are perfectly balanced and will always bring you back to balance and centeredness.

The celebrities have macrobiotic chefs because until you learn it, macrobiotic dishes and balanced menus are a bit complicated. You can learn from a book. Authorities suggest easing into it rather than "going whole hog." Start by committing to maximizing whole grains in the diet or introducing some macro dishes you love and building from there. You learn to respond to imbalances of feeling and energy with certain foods. It is helpful to have lessons though. I can obviously follow a recipe, but it was not until a macrobiotic cooking class that I finally perfected making miso soup that did not taste like boiled socks.

Attitude and attention to feelings and intention are involved, like cooking with love. We all know it is love that makes Mum's rhubarb crumble the best in the world, but how about packing a bean sprout salad for your lunch with love for yourself? You must make an occasion of meals and pay attention to the food and, famously, chew your mouthfuls a large number of times.

If you want to investigate further, I recommend Jessica Porter's *Hip Chick's Guide to Macrobiotics*, which is hilariously witty, and Verne Varona's *Dummy's Guide to Macrobiotics*, (Porter, 2004; Varona, 2009). The purist and classic works can be a little dry, but you will end up reading them once you are hooked. It sounds culty, but a two-week macrobiotic retreat left me feeling healthier than I had in years and really inspired me in all aspects of my life. Now I know, whatever ails me, be it- heartbreak or heartburn, miso soup is going to help, and when I start feeling yucky, the first thing to do is put on some brown rice.

Reiki

I AM NOT SURE IF REIKI relates to air energy exactly. Perhaps it is more etheric than airy, but this seems like the best spot for it. It is "out there", and that will appeal to many airy type people.

Reiki is a system of energy healing. It is an ancient practice which was rediscovered in Buddhist texts by a 19th century Buddhist monk in Japan. Practitioners of reiki completed 'attunements' to learn to strengthen and direct a universal healing energy, 'ki' ('rei' means boundless or universal). Anyone can use reiki techniques to good effect, but the energy transfers and special knowledge passed during a series of three 'attunements' with a reiki master will make the effects more powerful. The energy healing happens by the direction of ki via the placement of hands on specific parts of the body, usually while the client is lying down.

When you have a reiki treatment, you will typically feel the energy shifts that occur as stuck and toxic energies are released. It is common to have a feeling of coldness, slight trembling, or the intensification of something like a headache before the energy is released. Your reiki practitioner will encourage you to rest and allow these processes, and to drink plenty of water to assist the release. It is common to experience spontaneous and unexpected releases of emotion as tears or laughter without knowing why.

Reiki operates on the physical and etheric layers of your aura or energy fields, the two closest to the body. Integrated Energy Therapy is an allied practice that works in a similar way on the next more outer layers of the aura, invoking angels and angelic energy to assist in healing spiritual as well as emotional blockages.

Reiki can work extraordinarily well in conjunction with other healing modalities such as acupuncture, Bach flower essence therapy, shamanic work, or even psychotherapy, and helps the healing process be more rapid and effective. You are getting that etheric input as an adjunct to the physical shifts.

Soul/Spirit

Mindfulness

YOU CAN THINK OF MINDFULNESS as a type of meditation or perhaps as an aspect of meditation. It is about paying close attention to what is. You can be intensely aware of everything around you, the precise shade of yellow of a daffodil, the feel of a warm breeze on your skin, the sound of your footsteps in autumn leaves, the swish of car tires driving past you in the rain. You can focus inwardly on what you feel, the heaviness of tired muscles, the tightness of a slightly sunburned face, the sound of your breath, or the movement of your ribs as you breathe. In this action of bringing your awareness to what you are doing, seeing, or feeling, you are therefore not dwelling on the past or the future, which is usually what is at the root of anxieties. We agonize over the past which we cannot change, whether we made the right decisions, did the right thing, acted, or did not act as we should. We worry about a future when we cannot really know how things will work out or what other factors will come into play. Who considered the possibility of COVID-19 changing everyone's world? When we are 100 percent in the now, we are free of these anxieties.

How does it feel chopping these herbs? Drink in the scent of them. Feel the drag of the rake as you tidy up the leaves, smell the bonfire in a nearby garden, hear the blackbird's last song of the evening. Cultivating habits of mindfulness keeps you calm and tunes you into potential joy. The practice of mindfulness has been shown to have significant positive effects for depression and anxiety disorders, and even physical illnesses like irritable bowel syndrome and auto-immune conditions like fibromyalgia and myalgic encephalomyelitis.

And it just means doing what you already do but doing it in a more conscious way.

As the Buddhist aphorism goes, "Before enlightenment you chop wood and carry water, and after enlightenment you chop wood and carry water." Externally, nothing has changed, but internally, because you do the ordinary things of life with mindfulness, it is quite different. You are not doing chores with frustration, wishing you were doing something more important or momentous. You realize you are doing something fundamentally important, that you are blessed to have the strength and opportunity to do it. You can enjoy being outside and moving. You are not wasting psychic energy on the unchangeable past or the unknowable future but squeezing every drop out of real life in the now.

Reaching Out

ALL HUMAN BEINGS NEED social connections. Whether you are a "party animal" or a shyer and more introverted person, we all need to connect. If we are lucky, we are surrounded by family, friends, co-workers, and interact regularly with them. It is easy for connections to be broken if you must move to a new place, change jobs, or go through a major life challenge like illness or bereavement.

You can suddenly find yourself spending too much time alone, missing the companionship you have had in the past. Loneliness and isolation take a huge toll on health. In fact, loneliness can damage your health worse than smoking 100 cigarettes a week (Tate, 2018). So, if you find yourself in that situation, it is important to take action.

Rather than sitting at home alone after work, try to get involved in things that connect you to other people. Check out the clubs, classes, and activities that go on around where you live. Sign up for a class to learn something that appeals to you or volunteer for a cause or charity that you care about. Pick up the phone and call a friend or family member. If it occurs you have lost touch with people in general, reach out to old connections. Once I decided I would send out a postcard a week to all the people that I missed where I had an address.

Being alone in a new location is tough, and it can be hard to start feeling at home. Even simple things like holding the elevator for a neighbor, smiling, and saying hi, or offering to shovel snow or rake leaves or carry in groceries can be a small beginning to feeling you belong. In a new job, asking questions to know our new colleagues better, inviting people for a walk at lunchtime, or offering to bring someone a coffee is a brave first step.

Online interactions are not quite the same, so watch you do not slip into letting your computer and TV eat up every evening and weekend. Screens can get a bit addictive and numbing loneliness creeps up on you unless you make a decision to change that. If the prospect of doing that is too scary, ask for help. Find a way to reach out that works for you. The people you reach out to need it as much as you!

Giving

CONTRIBUTING TO YOUR community and society is another basic component of well-being. Nothing makes you feel good quite as much as giving. You do not have to give money; giving your time, attention, and respect is just as valuable.

Taking part in a charitable or humanitarian effort is its own reward. For years I volunteered to help a local business host a Christmas party for the elderly on Christmas Eve. It was invariably a high point of the season. It felt like a respite from the stress and materialism of the holidays and the joy and laughter, cheekiness and nostalgia of the guests was contagious and moving. You went home feeling you had really reconnected with the true "Spirit of Christmas," like Scrooge in Charles Dickens' *A Christmas Carol.*

There is so much need around us, even and perhaps very poignantly in the most affluent societies. People go hungry in prosperous wealthy cities. Food banks abound, and they need people to run them. There are children who need encouragement and opportunities to develop and reach their potential, and there are opportunities to volunteer in youth clubs or act as a mentor and profoundly change someone's life.

As well as contributing, the volunteer makes social connections to caring and giving people who share their values. They can also develop skills, such as organizing and communicating that will translate to other areas of their lives like work and study. Everyone wins.

Relationships as a Mirror

RELATIONSHIPS WITH others tend to be the highest and lowest experiences in our lives. The loss of a key relationship is painful and results in grief as acute as bereavement. The absence of partnership and close friendship can make life seem very empty and sad.

We can reach out and make connections, as we discussed above. In today's world, many search for a partner online, as well as meeting people in the traditional ways.

Once we have bonded with another, relationships take work, attention, and respect to remain healthy and successful. When we run into conflict, difficulty, or disappointment in relationships, the first step is a step back and a look at ourselves. Famously, we resent in others the traits and habits that we fail to recognize in ourselves. Maintaining a happy and healthy partnership, friendship, or relationship with a sibling requires us to know as much about ourselves as about them. We can come to learn about ourselves "in the mirror of relationship." It can be a bit of a minefield, but for most of us, it is worth it in the end.

Relationship therapy is there not just for couples trying to salvage and repair damaged relationships, but for single people too. In so many cases, when things go wrong in relationships, we can see associations or parallels in our relationships with our parents, or find we have erroneous or distorted beliefs and expectations about relationships based on the interactions we observed growing up. Are the relationships in your life good for you? Is your partnership helping or hindering your personal development or healing? If the answer is no, it is not necessarily the end of the road. Confronting and fixing issues can bring you closer and make you both able to be more supportive than ever.

For many people, the relationship with a pet is hugely important. You get to express love and devotion by the care you give them, and they repay you with their attachment and nonjudgmental affection. It is not the same challenge or reward that comes with human interactions, but it is significant. Dogs are exuberant in their devoted attachment and build a whole social world for you in your shared daily walks and interactions with other dog walkers. Owners of cats will know that the famed feline aloofness is just a 'front.' If your finances, schedule, and living situation make it feasible to own a pet, that can add a beautiful dimension to your life. There are a lot of eager candidates waiting at your local shelter.

Angels

DO YOU BELIEVE IN ANGELS? They are spiritual beings with a very high-vibration energy. They exist outside of our worldly constraints of space and time. Many of the world's religions embrace the idea of angels as benign and protective energies capable of interacting with people with and influencing human life. Interestingly, disparate, and seemingly unconnected faith traditions involve accounts of angels *with the same names.*

We describe and represent angels as ethereal, androgynous, winged beings, but that is for the purposes of understanding them within the restraints of human perception and understanding. There are types and hierarchies of angels: cherubim and seraphim and choirs, with arcane distinctions. Most people are aware of archangels such as Gabriel, who announced to Mary the future arrival of baby Jesus. In the Old Testament, Tobias is unknowingly accompanied by the archangel Raphael, who arrives to guide him to act to achieve healing for his father and family. Lots of people believe each has a personal guardian angel appointed to watch over us and protect and guide us in life. The Talmud, a Jewish sacred text describes how every blade of grass has its own angel, bending over it, whispering "Grow, grow!" in encouragement.

Angels intercede. They plead our case with the divine, and they intervene to alter events and situations beyond our control. They are healing and protective. However, angels are respectful of human free will and only intervene when they are asked. They are there waiting to be asked.

Another famous angel is one that was witnessed by many people, the Angel of the Somme who appeared after the most horrific and deadly battle in World War I. Stunned survivors, trying to take in the carnage and destruction they had witnessed, observed an all-encompassing golden light and were overtaken by an ineffable sense of peace that was healing to their broken and suffering spirits.

People attest to unknown or unseen agencies that intervene to inexplicably shield or protect them from harm in situations of danger. Others who have found themselves so stricken with pain and despair they feel they cannot continue suddenly find themselves lifted, carried, and soothed, and the pain is alleviated such that they make it through a dark passage in life. This mysterious help is attributed to angels.

You can invite angels into your life and ask for their help with anything. Simply calling on them will bring them to your side. Some people see visions of angels; others feel them touch their shoulders. These experiences can feel quite emotionally overwhelming, for we are in the presence of pure love. Others read signs of the presence of angels. One common sign is the appearance of a white feather or three white feathers. This is taken as the encouragement of angels, affirming that you are on the right path or as a sign to pay close attention to something significant that is occurring at that time that you should not miss.

A beautiful interpretation of angels is Wim Wenders' film *Wings of Desire,* which follows angels in their 'work' around the city of Berlin (Wenders, 1987). All interactions with angels are highly personal and working with them inevitably raises your energy vibration and inspires you to greater compassion and love.

Chapter 6: Earth: Ground Control

E arth energy is concerned with structure and stability. It deals in the real: things we can touch, taste, smell, feel and hear; things we can rely on. It builds things that are useful, practically, and materially. Of course, it connects to this beautiful world we inhabit and is deeply concerned to honor and protect nature.

Mind

Planning and Routine

A PERSON WITH A LOT of earth energy likes a bit of structure and predictability. We could all take a leaf from their book. There is the adage that "failure to plan is planning to fail." A timetable or schedule is not a straitjacket; it helps be organized in taking care of business. Knowing what we need to do and keeping up to date with tasks and responsibilities makes us more productive, demonstrates our effectiveness and reliability to others, and wins their support.

When work or domestic tasks or social obligations seem overwhelming, consider how you could organize better and see what difference that makes. Housework can be broken down into regular daily tasks. In fact, housework, done in a mindful, regular, and organized way can be quite soothing and meditative. Washing the dishes after dinner can be a time of quiet reflection and a wind down from a busy day. Manically carrying out a major spring clean the evening before a visitor arrives is stressful and exhausting. An environment that is clean and tidy all the time is relaxing and healing to be in, and visitors can arrive anytime. Big events are less of a strain if you start preparing well ahead and do as much as possible in advance. It conserves your energy for enjoying the celebration or gathering when it happens, instead of being a frazzled wreck.

Routines are the prosaic structure on which you can hang all the shiny and beautiful things in life. If you are taking care of things like health and work commitments and social and domestic responsibilities, you are free to add the spontaneous extras in life that brighten it up. You are not chasing your tail and playing catch up and can afford the time and money for a holiday or a treat.

Work and Money

WE SPEND SO MUCH TIME at work, we need to make sure it is working for our health and well-being. If we are lucky, our work is interesting and inspiring and enjoyable for us. If it is not that great, it can still be a positive force in that it pays our bills, gives a certain structure to life, gives us an identity, and makes clear our contribution to life and society.

If work is not working for you, it can be very debilitating and depressing. Ask for help and advice and try to figure out how you can make it better. Can you change your hours or location or role to make it more enjoyable? Can you work to repair or improve difficult relationships at work? Make use of work reviews to push for changes. Prepare well so you can back up what you are doing well for the company and then try to state, calmly and clearly, what you think would make things better. If the workplace is not open and supportive, perhaps you need to plan to move. Start from where you are, thinking of it as the springboard you need for the move to the next thing. Do you need to learn something new? Can you take on a responsibility or challenge that you can add to a CV? If you want promotion, how can you dress, communicate, and act like someone who should be in charge? Ask for training opportunities and volunteer for new projects and initiatives. It is easy to despair, but sometimes just an internal decision that you are going to leave a difficult job can make you feel better, even if you have to stay there until a better opportunity comes up. Do the best job you can in the poor circumstances and get systematic about changing things.

Money is a funny old thing, but even if it is "just an energy," it benefits from being handled in a structured, grown up, and responsible way. It can also be the source of a lot of anxiety which can obviously impact your health. It is amazing how many people operate with no planned budgeting, just reacting to the bills as they appear and hoping there is not too much month left at the end of the money.

The exercise of constructing a budget is always interesting. "I spend *how* much on groceries?" "Wow, *this* is how much goes out each month on entertainment subscriptions, petrol and car repairs, and phone costs!" It is unlikely you will go through this process without making immediate changes.

A habit of saving, however little, is so beneficial. A huge proportion of the population are "less than three paychecks from the street," which is scary to contemplate. Whatever little buffer you can set aside for a crisis could save you from great anxiety or worse. It even means when something special or exciting comes along that has cost involved, you are more likely to have the resources to avail of it.

A website like Money-Saving Expert or advice centers can educate about managing money, which really should be taught in schools (Lewis, n.d.). If you are in above your head, do not delay. Get help. There are charities and agencies that can help you get a grip on finances, so they do not cause grief and anxiety. When you reach out, you will find it is a common situation. Learn how to make money work for you; do not let it be the other way around. Life is about much more important things—mainly love, in fact.

Clearing and Decluttering

EARTHY PEOPLE MAY TEND to hang onto stuff. We all like stuff, of course. There are the practical things we need around, like washing machines, and cars, beds and bed clothes, sofas, and TVs. Then there are pictures, books, furnishings, and fabrics that are inspiring and uplifting. Then there are the emotional things: your baby's first shoes, photographs, the champagne cork from your 21st or your wedding, or the battered old biscuit tin that belonged to your grandmother, or the bus ticket from a wonderful date that you use as a bookmark. How sentimental are you?

All of those things have their own special value, but many of us find ourselves accumulating huge quantities of belongings and filling all our storage spaces, garages, or, madly, rented storage spaces with stuff we don't need, don't use, and probably don't remember we own. The ultimate first world problem.

Marie Kondo's bestseller *The Life-Changing Magic of Tidying* inspired a craze for achieving a more minimalist environment. She advised on how to sort and declutter, famously exhorting us to decide whether each object under consideration "sparked joy." William Morris said we should have nothing in houses that we do not "know to be useful or believe to be beautiful." While I could not follow all of Ms. Kondo's advice, such as the uniform folding and color filing of t-shirts and underwear, the purging or extraneous stuff is very freeing and liberating. If a wholesale dumping of clutter is emotionally overwhelming, you could try periodic skimming through, rather like an archeological dig, layer by layer. There is a psychological dimension. Holding on to stuff relates to holding on to old emotions and old situations that are better squarely left behind. A serious decluttering exercise will always result in positive life shifts that you might not recognize as being related. You are clearing what is holding you back in life. Also, there is something deeply satisfying about a neat, organized cupboard. My linen closet is a work of art, it is a pity this does not carry through the whole house!

Conservation and Protecting Treasure

EARTH PEOPLE DO HAVE a special connection to the past, and this can be expressed in healthy ways too. They like tradition and might be interested in history, ancestors, or ancient cultures. Preserving heritage as expressed in cultural traditions and buildings and structures matters because these things link people to their environment and community.

Important aspects of the past are all around us. Appreciating buildings and artifacts or earthworks and stone circles connects us to our history and identity and fosters a sense of belonging and an individual's place in the history of the world. Looking after, studying, and sharing knowledge about these things could be rewarding for an earth energy person, whether they are volunteering at a heritage site or studying local history or the meaning of mysterious ancient structures.

Body

Respecting All the Senses

OF ALL THE ELEMENTAL types, the Earthy people are most connected to their bodies. They are firmly 'grounded' and understand the world through their senses.

Earthy people need and appreciate touch more than anyone. They excel at massage and are very good to hug. They are just so very *there*. They may be acutely sensitive to the feel of things, hating scratchy or synthetic fabrics and needing to be warm and comfortable and well fed. Airy and fiery people can get so focused on moving and doing, these things can pass them by, while watery people can be caught up in emotion or lost in realms of escapist fantasy and lose touch with the senses.

Earth energy types often have a love of music and almost always a love of food. Through these senses, they connect very directly with the physical environment and are very in tune with the natural world. Nature is deeply calming and inspiring to them. Even an urban Earth type probably has a window box and makes a detour whenever possible to take in the park and the squirrels.

Aromatherapy might appeal given the connection to the olfactory sense (and frequent combination with massage). They are probably sensitive to the smell of things hating harsh or chemical smells.

All elemental types can benefit from paying attention to the senses and so connecting to the earth energy they do have. 'Grounding' is the experience of being strongly connected to the feelings in the body and aware of your connection to the ground beneath your feet. It counteracts being lost in your thoughts or drifting in the etheric realms of the unconscious or fantasy. You can counteract those wobbly and unstable states by consciously 'grounding' by focusing on your weight and the connection your body makes with the ground or furniture you are sitting on under the action of gravity. You can strengthen that connection by imagining roots growing out of your body deep into the earth, wrapping around deep buried boulders, contracting, and pulling you down. It is physically, mentally, and emotionally stabilizing. Practice it regularly so it becomes a familiar process. Grounding consciously is one of the best things you can do following a frightening or traumatic experience.

Massage

WE MENTIONED THE LOVE of touching above, and this makes therapeutic massage especially suitable for very earthy people, either as recipients of massage or being practitioners themselves. It also is the way for non-earthy people to reconnect with their bodies. Comfortable couches and essential oils and soft lighting will all appeal and heal.

Food and Healing

FOOD IS THE BEST MEDICINE. A focus on healthy eating and good quality food is the best defense against disease.

Obviously, we should try to maintain the best diet possible by educating ourselves and purchasing the best quality food we can and eating regularly and in the right quantities. If imbalance and disease does occur, it is possible that in addition to any medicine or treatment prescribed by our physician, there are dietary choices that can be made to support healing. A qualified nutritionist can work out a dietary protocol suitable for a person challenged by heart disease, a skin condition, an intestinal complaint, or cancer.

We can educate ourselves about the foods that are naturally antibiotic and antiviral, like garlic or ginger, foods that balance our blood sugar levels or counteract over-acidity. We all know about eating citrus fruits for the Vitamin C, but do we know where we are getting other vitamins and nutrients? Supplements are great for ensuring we get minimum amounts of nutrients, but they are not a substitute for a balanced, optimal diet.

Herbs and Healing

MOST OF THE WORLD RELIES on plant medicine. Only in the affluent west do we consider it quaint or old fashioned or a rediscovered tradition. In fact, a huge proportion of modern pharmaceutical drugs are derived from plants. The development of antibiotics and vaccines in the 20th century revolutionized medicine. Now we are encountering antibiotic resistance, and a global pandemic has reminded us of the fragility of life.

Animals instinctively know the plants to eat if they are feeling unwell. Our ancestors gathered and grew lots of plants for their therapeutic properties. Health food stores have taught us that we can drink chamomile tea for upset stomachs, valerian for anxiety, or lime flower tea for sleeplessness and migraines. The capabilities of herbal medicine are much more extensive, and there are university-trained and licensed practitioners working privately. They are trained to know when complaints are best addressed by hospitals and standard pharmaceutical medicine. Natural does not mean weak, and it does not mean safe. There are herbal remedies that need to be administered in carefully measured dosages and plants that interact with allopathic medicine. Herbal medicine can have brilliant results, especially with chronic conditions that resist standard treatment.

There are conditions and situations when you need modern medicine and then herbal protocols can support your healing. Trained herbalists know their limitations as well as their powers. Be prepared for herbal medicine to take a little time to show results. You might be taking 'tinctures,' which are alcohol-based concentrations of herbal remedies, or teas made from combinations for herbs for weeks sometimes before results are apparent. An herbalist works holistically and will take detailed history. They will then prescribe several herbs aiming to address all aspects of health, not just your presenting complaint. They are bringing the body back into balance.

There are several wonderful women's herbals. A modern classic is *Hygieia: A Woman's Herbal* (Parvati, 1979). A more contemporary excellent herbal is *Botanical Medicine for Women's Health* (Romm, 2017). Herbal medicine was traditionally practiced by women and was actively suppressed by the male-dominated medical establishment emerging from the 16th century. Traditional practice is rich in remedies that specifically address women's health issues like menstruation, pregnancy, and menopause. Women attended birth and death and had a wealth of knowledge for supporting our way into and out of this world. If you want a more general and lyrical introduction to beauty and the history and practice of herbalism, Elisabeth Brook's *A Woman's Book of Herbs* (1992) is very inspiring.

Bach Flower Remedies

BACH FLOWER REMEDIES were developed by Dr. Edward Bach in the 1930s. He created the essences by floating the flowers in spring water and thereby infusing the water with the 'essence' or spiritual nature of the flower. When you take them, the spirit of the flower communicates with your soul and so activates the healing at that level, which goes on to influence the emotional and the physical. The five-component "rescue remedy" is popular for emotional first aid in cases of trauma or anxiety. Bach flower remedies are not supported by the scientific establishment, who can see no possible agency for effects and found them ineffective in trials they carried out, but then how do you prove a connection between the spirit of a flower and your soul? They might work for you as healing remedies or adjunct supports for other therapies. Other modern ranges of flower essences have been developed to address contemporary concerns, some with ranges focusing on women's healing, for example Australian Bush Flower remedies.

Crystal Healing

ALL THE INNUMERABLE gemstones and crystals that are found in the earth are beautiful objects and have always been treasured. Stones like diamonds, emeralds, and sapphires are valued, not just for their appearance or rarity, but for their healing qualities. The crystalline structure that imparts the characteristic translucency, transparency, and color allows the stones to transmit, refract, and focus healing energy. Thus, when a healing stone is held or close by, energy is transmitted at the right frequency to the patient, and negative energies are released, the crystal is a conduit of healing energy.

Rose quartz is a powerful healer of a broken heart and attracts love by soothing and opening the heart chakra. Tiger's Eye is good for healing eyes. It also helps people with scattered thoughts to organize and focus their thinking and emotionally helps to repair self-esteem issues, as well as stimulating and releasing creativity. Aquamarine is mentally calming; on a physical level, it heals throat and thyroid complaints and balances glandular secretions, and on a spiritual level, it opens the person to clairvoyance and other psychic perceptions. Amethyst is another calming crystal that can help diffuse anger and alleviate anxiety. It promotes connection with divine energies and opens the third eye, so it can enhance intuitive insights; it is so powerful at this that it can facilitate "out of body" or astral travel experiences, so use it in this way only when you are ready for these experiences.

Crystal healers will prescribe gemstone companions for your healing journey. Healing treatments when a selection of crystals are placed on or around the body can encourage and facilitate healing shifts in energy. They also create 'elixirs' by direct and indirect methods that can be drunk or used in baths. Practitioners can carry out "space healing" by 'gridding' the area with strategically placed stones. Crystals used for healing need to be cleansed, dedicated and periodically 'recharged' by exposure to moonlight or cleansing in sea or spring water.

Small, polished crystals are readily available from mind body spirit retailers or online and you can experiment to see how this resonates with you very inexpensively.

Body Scan Relaxation

THE BODY SCAN IS A method for relaxing and releasing bodily and mental tension. Lying down, you simply think your way from the bottom to the top of your body. Focusing first on your toes, you become aware of them, checking how they feel. Then gently tense them and, with an out breath, actively release that tension and relax them. Continue to your foot, your ankle, your leg and so on. After one leg is attended to, switch to the other, then progress up the trunk of the body, across the intestines and stomach to the chest, the arms and the neck to the face, the forehead, the sides, back, to the top of the head. You can talk yourself through the process or listen to a recording. It is so effective, you are often fast asleep before then end, but that is allowed!

Spirit/Soul

Connecting to the Natural World

BEING IN TOUCH WITH our natural world is incredibly healing. Modern life can distance us from trees and grass, the sight and sounds of birds and animals, and even a true connection with the weather and seasons. If you are not lucky enough to live somewhere where you can get out into the wild, try to visit a park or pay special attention to the brave trees, plants, and animals that survive in our cities. Foxes and squirrels and pigeons are our urban wildlife; rats are less popular. London is lucky in having many big green spaces, celebrated as the "lungs of London," but even its most industrial and grimy places have some trees, often the amazing London plane tree, whose patchy bark peels away, helping it shed the toxins it absorbs from the polluted air. Plucky plants fight up through the concrete, cling to sides of buildings, and colonize the gutters.

You can create your own little Eden in a window box or on a balcony. There is something very wonderful about getting your hands muddy, planting things, and seeing them grow. You can even grow yourself some food. If it is your thing, allotments and community gardens connect people with plants and people. They are peaceful and relaxing, as well as bringing the benefits of being outside in the fresh air and digging and moving about.

Beekeeping is not just a rural pursuit either, with beehives in the most unexpected places in the heart or our big cities. Bees are essential to human life, pollinating the plants that give us two-thirds of our food. Also, bees are under threat from pesticides and pollution and their own pandemics, so keeping bees is an important way to save the world. Apart from being incredibly interesting, beekeeping is very calming and meditative. You must move slowly and calmly when you work with bees. You do get the occasional sting, inevitably, but you get used to it and these mild stings are part of the reason beekeepers stay active and agile to an old age. Apart from the fun of beekeeping, there is the honey and the wax and the propolis to gather.

Honoring and Protecting Gaia

YOU ARE CONNECTING to nature when you think in terms of conservation and climate change awareness. Recycling, choosing sustainable purchases, and protecting wild places and wildlife honors Mother Earth, or 'Gaia' as she is called. Education, activism, or volunteering in conservation organizations might be part of your path, being born at a critical point for the future of humanity and the safeguarding of our environment.

Nature Spirits

THE NATURAL WORLD HAS its own spiritual dimension. Every tree or rock or body of water has its own spirit or 'daemon.' The wild places are populated by these elemental beings. They include fairies of various types and nymphs, like the naiads that inhabit lakes and streams, the nereids in the seas and oceans, and the dryads that occupy trees. Fairies are very various, including elves, pixies, sprites, goblins, and numerous rare types specific to certain areas. Some are minute and appear like specks of light to those that can see them, and some are as tall as men or taller. Fairies are rather unpredictable and tricky. They can be helpful, but also mischievous. Above all, they expect to be treated with respect and can be very touchy, reacting to any perceived slight.

Connecting to fairies therefore is an unpredictable business. If you are in tune with the natural world, appreciate wildlife and wild plants, and try to protect them, the fairies will be predisposed to show themselves to you. Sometimes they will respond to wishes, especially those made at the propitious times, like May Eve or Midsummer's Eve when they are most visible. A gift will help; anything pretty or sparkly will appeal to them. A pearl button, a scrap of ribbon, or a crystal would all be acceptable. If you need help with an environmental concern, they are right behind you. One thing is for sure: if you want to connect you have to do it outside, speaking to them as you walk, run, or dance in nature, in woods, by the sea, or in the mountains. Some people see them; some just sense they are there.

Harmonia Saille gives an account of her connection with elementals. *Walking the Faery Pathway* is a how-to manual for you to follow (Saille, 2009). She explores the different fairies in countries across the world and reviews a range of elementals from mermaids and selkies, to undines and "trooping fairies" (they do road trips) to goblins, sylphs, and the *Bean Sidhe* or banshee. It also includes instructions on inviting them into your home or garden by creating a welcoming symbolic environment and decorating it with candles, crystals, and offerings of food. They love happy, dancing music too. "Fairy doors" placed in a garden will also be taken as an invitation.

To connect with fairies is to connect to the Goddess and be part of healing the divine feminine. The French singer-songwriter ZAZ has a beautiful song, "La Feé" (2010) which describes on one level the rescue of an injured fairy (as beloved by innumerable French children), but is also a metaphor for the life-limiting emotional damage experienced by a contemporary woman and the gentle healing offered by the solidarity of a woman friend who understands "she wants to fly, but can't" (yet).

The fairy faith is still strong in Celtic areas, like Brittany, Ireland, Scotland, Wales, and the Isle of Man. If this is your heritage, you may feel drawn to connect with the elementals. Some people retain a fear of fairies and seek to keep them away. They were blamed for illnesses in livestock, spoiled milk, or serious mischief like the theft of children. For some people, fairy places (like raths, fairy trees, ancient stone monuments) are places to fear; for others, they are a magnet. I think fairies behave well if you behave well to them and to the wild places where you live, and you can invoke their help with healing. Do you believe in fairies?

Conclusion

In the foregoing book, we have visited 53 ideas for growth and self-healing. They are intended to provide springboards for you to explore your own healing path. It is a lifelong process, remember. The practices you enjoy may naturally lead you deeper into them. They might also lead you to allied paths that will inspire. Remember to 'feed' all four of your elemental inner selves and all aspects of being, mind, body, and soul. You are changing and evolving all the time, very quickly once you embrace the conscious path to wholeness, so perhaps in six months' time the practices that seem too alien today will suddenly appeal. Joy on your journey!

Blessing

May you walk a path of healing
May it lead to light
May the journey be blessed
With love and laughter
With passion and inspiration
With friendship and belonging
And ever-increasing joy

References

Altman, G. (n.d.-a). *Woman.* In Pixabay.com. Retrieved September 12, 2020, from https://pixabay.com/illustrations/woman-silhouette-sunset-view-3918661/

Altman, G. (n.d.-b). *Woman silhouette flare joy.* In pixabay.com. Retrieved September 13, 2020, from https://pixabay.com/illustrations/woman-silhouette-flare-joy-person-2188033/

Angelo, J. (2002). *Spiritual healing.* Godsfield Press.

Bass, E., & Davies, L. (1988). *The courage to heal.* Harper and Row.

Bettelheim, B. (1976). *The uses of enchantment.* Thames & Hudson.

boaz. (2019, October 24). *Divine masculine and feminine energies.* Fourth Initiate. https://fourthinitiate.com/divine-feminine-and-masculine-energy/

Brand, R. (2017). *Recovery: Freedom from our Addictions.* Pan Macmillan.

Brooke, E. (1992). *A woman's book of herbs.* The Women's Press Ltd.

Brooke, E. (1993). *A woman's book of shadows*. The Women's Press Ltd.

Brown, B. (2011). *The power of vulnerability*. In TED (Ed.), YouTube. https://www.youtube.com/watch?v=iCvmsMzlF7o

Bull, A., & Walters, G. (Eds.). (2000). *Healing: an a-z guide to complementary medicine*. The Times.

Supplementary Series.

Cameron, J. (1992). *The artist's way: a spiritual path to higher creativity*. J.P. Tarcher.

Cameron, J. (1995). *The Artist's Way*. Pan Macmillan. (Original work published 1994)

Choquette, S. (2004). *Trust your vibes*. Hay House, UK.

Choquette, S. (2010). *Travelling at the speed of love*. Hay House, UK.

Coghill, R. (2000). *The healing energies of light*. Gaia Books.

Crisp, Q. (1986). *The wit and wisdom of Quentin Crisp* (G. Kettlehack, Ed.). Arrow Books Ltd. (Original work published 1985)

Croisy. (n.d.). *Forest Nymph*. In Pixabay.com. Retrieved September 13, 2020, from https://pixabay.com/photos/nymph-forest-nature-elf-beautiful-1052752/

Cunnigham, D. (1982). *Being a lunar type in a solar world*. Samuel Weiser.

Cunningham, S. (1982). *Magical herbalism.* Llewellyn.

de Beauvoir, S. (1949). *The Second Sex.* Gallimard.

Edwards, B. (1979). *Drawing on the right side of the brain.* J.P. Tarcher.

Emoto, M. (2001). *The hidden messages in water.* Sunmark Publishing, Japan.

Farmer, S. D. (2004). *Power Animals.* Hay House.

Femininity. (n.d.). Wikipedia. Retrieved September 5, 2020, from https://en.wikipedia.org/wiki/Femininity

Five steps to mental wellbeing. (n.d.). Www.Nhs.Uk. Retrieved September 1, 2020, from https://www.nhs.uk/conditions/stress-anxiety-depression/improve-mental-wellbeing/

Fontana, D. (2008). *The new secret language of dreams.* Duncan Baird.

Frankl, V. (1959). *Man's search for meaning.* Beacon. (Original work published 1946)

Giografiche. (n.d.). *Sky / Clouds.* In Pixabay.com. Retrieved September 12, 2020, from https://pixabay.com/photos/sky-clouds-rays-of-sunshine-weather-414199/

Goldberg, N. (2005). *Writing down the bones.* Shambhala Publications. (Original work published 1986)

Hamid, S. (2020). *Phases of the moon*. In Pixabay.com. https://pixabay.com/photos/ phase-of-the-moon-night-star-4969110/

Hay, L. L. (2004). *You can heal your life*. Hay House, UK. (Original work published 1984)

Honervogt, T. (2006). *Reiki for emotional healing*. Gaia Books.

Illes, J. (2004). *The element encyclopaedia of 5000 spells*. Harper Collins.

Jaugsberg, E. (n.d.). *Environmental protection*. In Pixabay.com. Retrieved September 12, 2020, from https://pixabay.com/photos/ environmental-protection-326923/

Jeffrey E., Y., & Janet S., K. (1994). *Reinventing Your Life*. Penguin Group (USA).

Keller, S. (n.d.). *Waterfall*. In pixabay.com. Retrieved September 10, 2020, from https://pixabay.com/photos/ waterfall-wave-fantastic-woman-2271231/

Kipling, R. (1910). *Rewards and Fairies*. Macmillan & Co.

Kondo, M. (2014). *The life-changing magic of tidying up*. Random House. (Original work published 2011)

Lee, A. (Director). (2000). *Crouching tiger, hidden dragon*. [Film].

Lee, N. (2018, January 4). *5 proven ways to set goals and achieve them.* Medium. https://medium.com/swlh/5-proven-ways-to-set-goals-and-achieve-them-cf19016b3af1

Lewis, M. (n.d.). *moneysavingexpert.com.* Retrieved September 12, 2020, from https://www.moneysavingexpert.com/

Low Dog, T. (n.d.). *Life is your best medicine.* Retrieved September 1, 2020, from https://www.pdfdrive.com/life-is-your-best-medicine-a-womans-guide-to-health-healing-and-wholer

MiraCosic. (n.d.). Astrology. In *Pixabay.com.*

Moran, C. (2011). *How to be a woman.* Penguin Random House, London.

Nuur, D. (n.d.). *Balancing your masculine and feminine energies.* Goop.Com.

Parvati, J. (1979). *Hygieia: a woman's herbal.* Wildwood House.

Pinkola Estes, C. (1992). *Women who run with the wolves.* Random House.

Porter, J. (2004). *The hip chick's guide to macrobiotics.* Penguin.

Restall Orr, E. (2000). *Ritual: a guide to life, love and inspiration.* Harper Collins.

Robinson, S., & Corbett, T. (1987). *The Dreamer's Dictionary.* Grafton. (Original work published 1974)

Rogers, V. (2000). *Your handwriting can change your life.* Simon and Schuster.

Romm, A. (2017). *Botanical medicine for women's health.* Churchill Livingstone.

Russell, S. (Director). (2007, July 31). *The barefoot doctor's tai chi workout.* [DVD]. Barefoot Doctor.

Rustamov, K. (n.d.). *Girl Ninja Hands.* Retrieved September 8, 2020, from https://pixabay.com/images/search/girl%20ninja%20hands/

Saille, H. (2009). *Walking the Faery Pathway.* John Hunt.

Sparkler. (n.d.). In pixabay.com. Retrieved September 12, 2020, from https://pixabay.com/photos/sparkler-holding-hands-firework-677774/

Tate, N. (2018, May 4). *Loneliness rivals obesity, smoking as health risk.* https://www.webmd.com/balance/news/20180504/loneliness-rivals-obesity-smoking-as-health-risk

Thoele, S. P. (2001). *The courage to be yourself.* Conari Press. (Original work published 1991)

Varona, V. (2009). *Macrobiotics for dummies.* Wiley.

Wenders, W. (Director). (1987, May 17). *Wings of desire.* [Film].

Wilde, O. (1895). *The importance of being earnest.* [Play.]

Yin yang abstract symbol. (n.d.). In Pixabay.com. Retrieved September 24, 2020, from https://pixabay.com/illustrations/yin-yang-abstract-background-black-99824/

ZAZ. (2010). *La Feé* [Song]. https://www.youtube.com/watch?v=4l0ge5UnuuA